CAREERS IN
TEACHING

BY
GLEN W. CUTLIP
AND
ROBERT J. SHOCKLEY

The Rosen Publishing Group, Inc.
NEW YORK

Published in 1994, 1997, 2000 by The Rosen Publishing Group, Inc.
29 East 21st Street, New York, NY 10010

Cover Photo © Evan Johnson/Impact Visuals

Revised Edition 2000

H.S. ¹⁄₀₀ 16.95

Library of Congress Cataloging-in-Publication Data

Cutlip, Glen W.
    Careers in teaching/by Glen W. Cutlip and Robert J. Shockley
rev. ed.
        p. cm.
    Includes bibliographical references and index.
    ISBN 0-8239-3182-X
    1. Teaching—Vocational guidance—United States—Juvenile literature. I. Shockley, Robert J., 1921–. II. Title.
LB1775.2.C88 1993
3709.23973—dc20   93-5887
                                                                        CIP
                                                                        AC

Manufactured in the United States of America

About the Authors

Dr. Glen W. Cutlip holds a doctorate from West Virginia University. He has pursued advanced study in public administration, most recently at The Johns Hopkins University, Baltimore, Maryland.

Dr. Cutlip taught language arts in the public schools of West Virginia before moving into community college teaching. Later he joined the West Virginia Department of Education as a reading curriculum specialist. He then became a branch chief in the Maryland State Department of Education. Currently Dr. Cutlip is a senior policy analyst at the National Education Association in Washington, DC.

Dr. Robert J. Shockley received his MA and EdD degrees from Teachers College, Columbia University. His teaching career includes several years in a private school in New York City and additional experience in the public schools of Baltimore County, Maryland. He also was a consultant in the education department of the Glenn L. Martin Company.

Dr. Shockley spent his administrative career in the public schools of Maryland, as a principal, assistant superintendent, director of curriculum, and special assistant to the superintendent of schools. He has traveled extensively throughout the world, and he served as an evaluator of the Teacher Corps Project in Nepal. He is now retired and devotes his time to consultant work, writing, travel, and golf.

Acknowledgements

This book is dedicated to our families and colleagues, without whose patience and understanding the completed manuscript would not have been possible.

We wish to thank James Sherwood and the Prince George's County (Maryland) Public Schools for their input for this edition.

We also appreciate David W. Hornbeck for providing the foreword for this book. Hornbeck served as the state superintendent of schools in Maryland and as president of the Council of Chief State School Officers. He is one of the most noted authorities in educational reform, specifically in the areas of accountability, special education, and education of the disadvantaged. Several state legislatures have used him as a consultant in drafting education reform legislation. He is currently superintendent of the Philadelphia public school system.

Contents

Foreword   *vi*

1. Considering Teaching for Your Career   *1*
2. Teaching Is a Professional Career   *9*
3. Preparing to Become a Teacher   *14*
4. Getting a Professional License and
   Certification   *35*
5. Beginning Your Career in Teaching   *44*
6. Continuing in Professional Practice   *75*
7. Emerging Challenges in Teaching   *99*
8. Your Exciting Future in Teaching   *102*

Glossary   *107*

Appendix
   I. Directory of State
      Teacher Certification Agencies   *110*
   II. Education-Related Organizations   *121*

For Further Reading   *134*

Index   *136*

Foreword

Astronaut Christa McAuliffe said, "I touch the future. I teach." There is no more noble or rewarding profession.

Do you believe that the next generation should think more critically, more analytically? If so, consider teaching!

Do you believe that human beings should demonstrate more often and more deeply that caring about other human beings is one of our highest virtues? If so, consider teaching!

Are you concerned that our prison population and our welfare rolls are expanding? If so, consider teaching! Do you or people you know worry that our capacity to blow up the world may someday become a reality? If so, consider teaching!

Do you hope that your children will have the best that life on this planet can offer? If so, consider teaching! The ripple effect resulting from one good teacher— perhaps you, the reader—can change a life, save a community, enlighten a nation, lead a world to peace. Take up the challenge. Consider teaching!

David W. Hornbeck
Superintendent
Philadelphia Public Schools

1

Considering Teaching for Your Career

It is not unusual to have questions and doubts about the choice of a career. You have already been exposed to many choices, through family, the media, and school, and the idea of becoming a teacher will probably be just another in a long list of possibilities for your future. A good place to start, however, is to ask yourself some hard questions:

- Does the possibility of spending many years in an academic environment appeal to me?
- Do I enjoy working with others to help them gain more knowledge and skills?
- Do I have the personality and desire to become a successful teacher?

DECIDING ON YOUR CAREER

One of the best ways to begin answering these career questions is to read books like this one to find out all you can about teaching and related careers.

Another important step is to use your eyes and ears. Ever since you first entered school, you have been exposed to many teachers and have formed strong opinions on what you liked and did not like about the way they taught. You can use the months ahead to sharpen your observation skills, paying particular attention to how your current teachers carry out their assignments and whether or not they seem happy in their work.

Also, consider talking to some of your teachers about why and how they chose teaching as a career, and what they consider to be the weak and strong points of the work. If your teachers are like those who have responded to national surveys, you will find that they generally are satisfied with their careers and would still choose teaching if they had the choice to make all over again. They will highlight the joys of seeing students grow in skills, and they will tell you that they enjoy the constant challenges that teaching presents.

Characteristics of Quality Teachers

Which of your teachers would you rate as the very best? What personal and professional qualities does he or she have that prompted you to think that? The following traits are generally accepted by administrators, teachers, and other students as those possessed by quality teachers:

A quality teacher is really interested in students.
Depending on the grade level and subject being taught, teachers face the challenge of teaching from 25 to 150 or more students daily. A skilled teacher is interested in each student and relates to each one as an individual. He or she inspires students to reach for his or her potential.

A quality teacher is an expert in a subject field and can relate it to other subject areas.
As a result, he or she speaks with authority. On the other hand, a good teacher can also admit not knowing the answers to questions.

A quality teacher uses a variety of teaching methods.
These techniques help students learn more quickly and effectively: lectures, demonstrations, audiovisual aids, and computer applications. The teacher not only knows what students need to learn but also is able to adapt teaching methods to the students' learning styles.

A quality teacher is a well-rounded individual.
Students characterize their best teacher as a "real person." He or she is actively involved in other areas—as class or club sponsor, sports coach, or participant in professional, religious, political, or community affairs. He or she is enthusiastic, firm but fair with students, and able to admit being wrong, and has a good sense of humor.

A quality teacher keeps up-to-date in all areas of the profession.
The best teacher is involved with refresher courses, visits to business and industry conferences, visits to other classrooms, and professional reading. He or she makes extensive use of state-of-the-art materials and is willing to try new methods.

A quality teacher has a keen understanding of his or her own strengths, weaknesses, likes, dislikes, and aspirations.
He or she can readily observe the growth patterns in students and analyze roadblocks to progress.

GETTING HELP WITH YOUR CAREER DECISION
You have done some reading on the career of teaching. You have looked at the best qualities of the teachers you like, and you think you might be right for the job. What are some other ways you can explore this decision?

Talk it over with your parents.
You may have thought about a variety of possible careers ever since you were in elementary school. It is also likely that your parents have made career suggestions to you. Now that you are getting closer to making a decision concerning college, it is a good idea to share your aspirations, plans, thoughts, concerns, and questions with your parents in more detail.

Share with your parents the insights you gain from this book and other career material that you read. You will probably have material from the guidance office, including career surveys, computer data, and information about colleges. Your family's financial situation is also an important part of the discussion.

In considering your parents' advice, remember that it is your future that is under discussion. Your parents need to know that you will choose a field of work that is both challenging and enjoyable to you.

Seek help from your school's guidance department.
Your guidance counselor already has a great deal of information about you as a background for discussion of your future plans. Your file probably includes your grades, attendance record, notations concerning any unusual behavior, achievement and aptitude test scores, PSAT and SAT scores, club memberships, awards and honors, and comments from teachers.

Most guidance counselors have additional tools to help you. They may arrange for you to take a career assessment survey covering topics such as occupations that interest you, your favorite subjects, future plans, your personal values, and your abilities.

In addition to books, brochures, and catalogs, computer programs are available that give information about colleges. Some colleges have produced films or videos that give you a tour of the campus. Armed with these tools, plus expertise as a good listener, your guidance counselor is in an excellent position to help you refine your career decision.

Read about the career.
In addition to books like this one, your guidance department and school library should have brochures and pamphlets describing a variety of careers. Excellent materials on teaching are available from the Future Teachers of America (FTA), the National Education Association (NEA), the NEA Student Program, and the U.S. Department of Education. Your state's department of education is another source of information, and many states have initiated programs to encourage students to consider teaching as a career.

Your counselor, parents, or school administrator can help you to make arrangements with a nearby school or college (or other classes in your own school) that teaches the grade level or subject that interests you. You may also want to sit in on other grades or classes in your own school. Try to visit actual classes in session and talk to the teachers. Ask the same kinds of questions you have asked teachers in your own school.

Activities That Will Help with Your Career Decision
Many opportunities are available to you right now, before you enter college, that will help to broaden your background of experience. These activities include part-time employment, volunteer work, internships, and participation in clubs and hobbies. Participation in such activities will help you to confirm your career decision,

gain "real-life"experience in areas related to teaching, and earn money toward college or university expenses.

The experiences that will be most helpful are those that give you practice with the skills you will need as a teacher. You might give serious thought to activities that involve dealing with people, answering questions, giving explanations and directions, giving actual instruction, or working with different age groups.

Among the activities that could help you with your career goals, consider the following:

Participate in club activities in your school.
Active participation, either as a member or an officer, will give you leadership experience and an opportunity to work on projects to improve the school. Do not overlook the Future Teachers of America (FTA). This organization will help you to become better acquainted with the teaching profession.

Become a volunteer.
Many organizations need volunteers, including church groups, Little League teams, Scouts, summer recreation programs, and nursing homes.

Get a part-time job.
Part-time employment can provide savings toward college expenses.

Find a summer job.
Summer camps and recreation departments have counselor-type positions available for qualified high school students.

Be a baby-sitter.
Many young people use baby-sitting both as a source of income and an opportunity to find out whether they enjoy working with young people.

Become a tutor.

Many schools provide opportunities for students to tutor other students who need extra help, particularly in mathematics and science. In most situations, this volunteer service improves the grades of both the tutor and those receiving help.

Apply for a student internship.

Many high schools offer top students the opportunity to become a teaching assistant through a student internship program. Interns handle routines for the teacher such as setting up and cleaning lab equipment, assisting with grading papers, doing clerical jobs, and operating audio-visual equipment. Some of these programs offer credits. The main advantages, however, are the opportunity to get a behind-the-scenes look at teaching and the experience of working closely with an excellent teacher.

Become a guide.

Many communities have historic sites, museums, or specialized parks that use guides.

Work with senior citizens.

Some hospitals and nursing homes have established volunteer programs that enable high school students to work with the elderly.

Find a new hobby.

Hobbies expand your experiences and fields of interest.

Start a collection.

Some of your teachers may have enriched your classroom experiences by sharing items from their own collections—perhaps slides from foreign travels, coins or stamps, or a first-edition rare book. Consider either enlarging a current collection or starting a new one that will give you both enjoyment and the possibility of enriching the experiences of your future students.

Volunteer for jobs in medicine.
Many hospitals have openings for candy stripers or lab or research assistants.

Take concurrent college courses.
If your school system has a cooperative program with local colleges or universities to allow high school students to take a college course, you should consider this activity, particularly if college teaching is your career choice.

Take part in a student-exchange program.
If you plan to choose either a foreign language or social studies as your major, you should consider this activity.

Continue and expand your reading.
Your success in college will depend both on how well you read and what you read. Choose a variety of books to read and set goals for yourself in terms of aiming to complete many of the classics.

If you take advantage of these types of opportunities right now, before your classes as a college freshman begin, you will have gained a head start in many of the key areas that are important for success as a teacher.

2

Teaching Is a Professional Career

Can you think of some of the largest traditional businesses in the United States? If you thought of names such as General Motors, Sears, Wal-Mart, Exxon, or AT&T, you are on the right track. These businesses have billion dollar budgets and many national offices or stores, and they employ thousands of people. You might be surprised, however, to know that the budget for the education of children in the United States is larger than almost any traditional business in this country. In fact, the total cost of operating schools in every community in the United States exceeds the money spent on national defense. Education costs are almost half of each state governor's budget every year. Thus, teaching can be thought of as a very large enterprise or business. Although a single group or person does not own education in the United States, the combined resources devoted to educating children make teaching a very large profession.

SCOPE OF THE PROFESSION

Let's look at the enormity of the education system in this country for a moment. The educational enterprise starts in the early morning with elaborate school bus

9

schedules to transport a significant portion of more than 52 million students in the public and private schools of the United States, not counting approximately 14 million students in college. Slightly more than 113,000 schools provide classroom space, and many schools even provide a breakfast program. The salaries of nearly 2.3 million teachers constitute the major portion of the educational budget, and do not overlook the cost of cafeteria, maintenance, and transportation services. After six or seven hours in the school day, the afternoon continues with intramural and interscholastic sports, clubs, laboratory experiences, adult education, and community programs. At the close of the regular school day, the busing schedules are reversed and students are transported home. It's quite an operation. Now add the students who are attending colleges and universities, and you can see that education is big business!

Also, take a look at the government structures needed to operate such an undertaking. Education is a function of each state because the Constitution does not specifically delegate the responsibility. Thus, the federal role in education has always been slight in the overall budget—approximately 6.2 percent. However, the federal government has played a very significant role in education by concentrating funds on programs for students with specific needs, such as those with disabilities or impoverished backgrounds. Examples of such current federal programs include Head Start, Chapter I, Education of the Handicapped, Adult Education, and Vocational Education. If you need financial assistance to attend college, federal programs for higher education will be significant in your future.

The federal government also sponsors research and development laboratories and assistance agencies for schools.

At the state level, any governor or state legislator will tell you that education is probably the largest budget item each year for the state. States normally use property taxes to help fund schools. A state board of education is usually appointed by the governor to oversee the schools at the state level. In some states, the state board appoints a state superintendent; in others the superintendent is elected by popular vote to be the chief administrative officer. The state superintendent in turn hires a staff in the state department of education to assist in monitoring the schools and providing assistance and leadership as necessary.

Within states, local political jurisdictions such as counties and cities have the responsibility to assess taxes and operate the schools on more of a day-to-day schedule. These local jurisdictions appoint or elect a school board of citizens to oversee the schools. Again the local school boards can appoint or elect a district superintendent to be the chief administrative officer of the schools. The local board and the superintendent organize the school and hire instructional and administrative staff to teach the students. Each school has a principal and teachers supported by district central office personnel.

Many schools then operate elaborate parent involvement programs, usually called the Parent-Teacher Association (PTA). You can see the complexity, enormity, and importance of the governmental task of educating the nation's children.

THE CHANGING PROFESSION

The teaching profession is continually changing. One significant change is that teachers are becoming more active in programs dealing with school-based decision-making. Teachers are also more educated, with more than half now holding either a master's degree or a doctorate.

The population served by teachers also is changing. Sixty-five percent of public school students are white, 16.8 percent of students are African-American, 13.5 percent are Hispanic, 3.7 percent are Asian American or Pacific Islanders, and 1.1 percent are American Indian. Teachers must be prepared to teach students with different backgrounds in culture, language, and religion.

Major changes in society have also affected the teaching profession. The rapid increase in the number of students entering school created a demand for many more teachers, and women filled that gap. The wars that took the male population in other directions swelled the female teaching ranks. Unfortunately, the lower pay usually given to working women throughout history increased the teaching ranks at the expense of women and the status of the profession. It was not until the late 1950s that men again came into the teaching force in large numbers. They tended to become secondary and college teachers and school administrators.

Of the more than 2.3 million teachers in the United States, almost 75 percent are female. At the elementary school level, 85 percent are female. At the secondary level, the ratio of women to men is closer to equal:

	Men	Women
Middle and Junior High School	35%	65%
High School	53%	47%

Statistics also point to the fact that teaching is an "aging profession" (the average age is now forty-three). This creates two problems: (1) a large number of teachers will be eligible for retirement at a time when there will be fewer qualified replacements; and (2) experienced teachers earn higher salaries than do new teachers. This imbalance, with a large proportion of the teachers at or near the top of the salary scale, causes school district budgets to balloon out of proportion.

The bad news is that a sluggish economy beginning in the late 1980s forced school districts to make substantial cuts in their budgets.

The good news is that teacher shortages in certain areas are attracting students into teacher-training programs. Shortages exist in ESL/bilingual education, special education, mathematics, science, foreign languages, and computer education. The nation experienced a minor baby boom, which has already begun to make an impact on enrollments in middle and high schools. Additional teachers will be needed to handle this surge in student populations for the next few years.

Now, as we enter the twenty-first century, the purposes, funding, and results of education are being reassessed. The teaching profession is also undergoing a profound reexamination. Teachers are optimistic that this reexamination will lead to lasting improvement.

Preparing to Become a Teacher

The previous chapters gave some guidance in deciding if teaching is the career for you. The following sections discuss how to select the appropriate college and/or route to becoming a full-fledged member of the profession.

Various routes will lead you to your destination. These routes generally fall into the following approaches:

Attend a major university with an education department.
This approach will provide you with a quality education and teachers' training.

Attend a state-supported or private teachers' college.
This approach will provide a quality education and teachers' training if you select the school carefully. The costs at state-supported schools are often lower than at major universities.

Attend a junior or community college for the first two years and then transfer to either type of school mentioned above.
This approach may help you financially during the first couple of years.

Attend a liberal arts college for four years and then obtain a master's degree in teaching.
This approach will provide you with an excellent education and allow career decisions to be postponed.

Take alternative certification programs.
These programs provide other routes to becoming a teacher, which will be discussed in detail in the next chapter.

In this chapter, we will concentrate on the traditional routes to a teaching career outlined in the first three approaches above.

APPLYING FOR ADMISSION
Researching prospective colleges should begin at the latest in your junior year of high school because applying for admission and taking the entrance examinations begin in the spring of that year. Your high school guidance counselor can give you practical advice on this matter. In addition, most colleges will not accept your application unless you have recommendations from people such as your guidance counselors, teachers, or principal, so you will want to start the application process early. The following are general admission requirements for most education colleges:

1. Graduation from an accredited high school. In some cases another type of high school certification, such as General Equivalency Diploma (GED), will suffice, particularly for persons beyond the typical high school age.
2. Recommendations from your high school teachers.

3. Completion of a well-balanced curriculum in high school.

Check with the college you are interested in attending about whether or not foreign languages, computer science, or other skills are necessary for entrance. These programs may be labeled "advanced" or "college-bound." They are not necessarily mandatory, but they receive preference from most college admissions offices. Colleges often accept promising students on the understanding that a deficit in any entrance requirement will be completed during the first year.

How Should You Select a College or University?

If you have made your decision to become a teacher, you should begin at once to narrow down your choices of a college or university. The logical place to begin your research on colleges is your school's guidance office. That office should have a supply of college catalogs and access to computer programs that can provide information on any school you might consider. Make an early appointment with your counselor to begin the information-gathering part of your search.

Another major resource for information on colleges and universities is your local library. Ask the librarian about any books or CD-ROMs that will help you with your research.

Practical Considerations

Cost

This is probably the most basic consideration. Can you and your parents afford the college tuition?

Distance from Home

Although you might be accepted for admission to the "school of your dreams," you will want to go home for vacations and certain family occasions. Traveling expenses will add additional costs to your college budget.

Your Grades, Courses Taken in High School, and ACT or SAT Scores

Your cumulative grade point average in high school and your scores on national tests have a large bearing on whether or not you are accepted by the college of your choice. Check carefully to make certain that you satisfy all entrance requirements.

Curricular Offerings

Check college catalogs and computer printouts to make certain that the college or university of your choice offers the programs in which you are interested.

Size of School

For some students, school size doesn't matter. Others feel more comfortable at a smaller school where they can have a greater feeling of belonging.

Class Size

Many students do better work in smaller classes and in situations in which they can be assured of individual attention.

Reputation of School

Although this quality is often subjective, it is important to know that the school you choose has a solid reputation.

School Accreditation

You should make sure that the teacher training program you choose is accredited by a recognized body such as the state, regional boards, or nationally by the National Council for Accreditation of Teacher Education Programs.

Housing

Many schools require freshmen to live in dormitories. This may be considered either desirable or undesirable by you and your parents. Whether your housing is on or off campus, you need to know that housing is readily available.

Scholarships

For many students, getting a scholarship makes the difference between one college and another.

Availability of Part-Time Work

Although part-time work puts an added strain on most students, it also can make it financially possible to attend the college of your choice.

Placement Office

Finding a job when you graduate may seem far in the future, but it is important to know that your college or university has an active placement office to help you in finding your first teaching position.

Extracurricular Activities

Many students feel that it is important for their college to have active sports, fraternity, sorority, and cultural activities to make up a well-rounded campus life. Participation on a varsity team also might make it possible to secure either a full or partial scholarship.

Student Loans
Another means of financial help is the student loan, available through sources such as the Carl D. Perkins National Direct Student Loan Program, state-operated programs, or loans administered by the college.

Financial Aid Earned Through Military Service
The military services make funds available for college to those who have served in the armed forces.

Preference to Family Members of Graduates
Some colleges and universities give special entrance consideration to students who are related to alumni.

Narrowing Down Your Choice
Having studied the practical considerations, you should have a better idea of the size and general location of the school you would like to attend. The Guidance Information Program (GIP), Discover Program, or similar program in your guidance office can provide the next logical step in helping you to gather specific information on colleges in the geographic area you have selected. These programs will provide a printout on school enrollment, median SAT scores, tests required for entrance, application deadline, tuition fees, and cost of room and board. The Discover Program and another program, Computer Assisted Scholarships for Higher Education (CASH), can supply you with information on financial aid programs available to college students. In addition, several private businesses offer to search for financial aid for you. If you are paying a fee, be a careful consumer.

When you have narrowed your choices to five or fewer schools, write to those schools immediately to request a catalog and current information on admission, financial aid, and scholarships.

Next Steps

The information you receive from the schools will enable you to begin an elimination process leading to your first, second, and third choices of schools. You should seriously consider applying to three schools, in case you are turned down by your first or second choice. Careful study of the materials will also prepare you for the following actions:

Keep your guidance counselor up-to-date.
At this point, he or she probably will give you a checklist to help you plan for becoming a college freshman. Check with your counselor as often as necessary to keep the lines of communication open and to make sure you have completed all of the necessary steps.

Talk to your parents.
Your parents also have a deep interest in your choice of schools. Seek their advice and keep them fully informed.

Attend a Career College Fair.
Most school systems hold an annual Career College Fair, giving juniors and seniors an opportunity to talk with representatives of colleges and universities, the military, and business and industry.

Talk to graduates.
Your counselor can help you identify graduates of your high school who are now attending the colleges you are considering. Get in touch with these students to ask what the college is really like.

Watch videos.
Some colleges and universities have produced videos describing life on the campus and other related information. Write to the school to find out whether a video is available.

Visit the campus.
The best way to determine your top choice of schools is to visit the campus. Ideally, this visit should be made with your parents or guardian. Most schools welcome the opportunity to host visitors. During a campus visit, you will probably be given printed information, be shown an audiovisual presentation, be assigned a student guide for a campus tour, and have the opportunity to talk to a representative of the college.

Final Steps in the Selection Process
After you have done the necessary reading, talking, and visiting, the final steps in the process depend largely on paperwork and the following important factors:

- Do your national test scores and your grade point average meet the minimum standards of the college or university?
- Do you have a financial plan (including scholarship, loan, or part-time employment) that will enable you to meet the cost of at least the first year?
- Will the school consider you a well-rounded person by your participation in extracurricular activities?

The following are generally accepted steps in the college admission process:

- Choose a major field in college. (Your choice of teaching as a career may already fulfill this requirement.)
- Limit your choice of college or university to three possibilities. (You should have completed this step.)
- Take the national tests that are required (for example, SAT, ACT, ACH) by your three schools.
- Complete the application for admission to your three schools. You need to include a transcript of your work in high school; in addition, many schools require recommendations from your principal, former employer, and at least one other staff member from your school.
- Await responses from your three schools. (For most students, this is the hardest part of the process!)
- Make your final choice from the schools that have accepted you. (This is the moment toward which you have been working!)
- Send a letter of acceptance to the college or university that you choose.
- Send letters of refusal to the schools that you do not choose. This is important in order to enable the schools to make their plans for other students.
- Send your final transcript to the college you choose.

HOW MUCH WILL YOUR TRAINING COST?

Fixed Costs

The type of college that you select and the standard of living you expect to have are the two major variables that determine the cost of your college education. Let us look at the first variable: the college you select.

Basically, three types of colleges offer teacher training programs that are accredited by state departments of education and other regional and national accrediting bodies. These college types are:

- Public teacher colleges
- State-supported universities
- Private colleges and universities

Each type of college or university has its strong points when you study academic programs. Public teachers' colleges have a long history of concentrating the bulk of their resources on teacher-training. They are state-supported and accredited and attract the majority of their students from within the state for a quality bachelor's degree at a reasonable price. The state-supported university also attracts students from within the state and complies with all teacher training accrediting requirements in offering a quality program. It is usually much larger than a teachers' college, and its tuition and costs are slightly higher. It offers a number of majors, such as science, engineering, medicine, and law; education is only one of many departments.

The private college or university often concentrates on providing a broad range of programs in the liberal arts, with teacher training as a smaller program. The private school typically provides a quality education in a broad range of subjects. Let's look at some comparative costs among these types of colleges.

FIXED EXPENSES

	Public Teachers' Colleges	State Universities	Private Colleges or Universities*
Tuition	$2,624	$4,168	$11,999
Room and board	4,808	5,460	5,510
Student fees (athletics, activities, health)	760	780	795
TOTAL	$8,192	$10,408	$18,304*
Out-of-state fees	3,476	10,220	0

*The costs for tuition, room, and board at the nation's most selective schools can run as high as $29,900.

You can see the wide range of options available in the basic fixed costs of college. These fees are due before enrollment each year; however, most colleges now accept credit cards and payment plans. The room and board fees are for students who choose to live on campus in a dormitory and eat in the cafeteria. Many colleges and guidance counselors recommend that your first year be spent in a dormitory, to help you get used to college life and to take full advantage of the college's resources. Costs can sometimes be reduced by living off campus with roommates.

Other Costs

Your style of living will greatly affect the other costs of attending college. Allowances for recreation and spending money, laundry, transportation, books and supplies, and clothes are the major expenses that relate to personal preferences. Although these are difficult to determine, the following is a yearly estimate by type of college. Such expenses can be reduced by economizing, buying used books, carpooling, and the like.

OTHER COSTS

	Public Teachers Colleges	State Universities	Private Colleges or Universities
Spending money and recreation	$1,620	$1,800	$1,980
Books and supplies	700	750	760
Laundry	170	180	210
Clothes	400	540	650
Transportation	500	560	740
TOTAL	$3,390	$3,830	$4,340

Financial Assistance

The ever-increasing cost of college education has been a topic of concern for more than two decades. Federal assistance programs have been developed, some of which are still in operation. Colleges have instituted installment plans, and a variety of advance-payment plans have appeared in many states. These programs are designed to raise revenue for the colleges and, at the same time, to give students and their parents some choices in paying for the cost of education.

Lack of money should not be the sole reason for not attending college. If you have the desire to succeed in your studies, you should explore the following financial assistance strategies. College catalogs and computer programs in your guidance office list costs, types of financial assistance available, and the process for applying for assistance. Early application is essential. The general categories of financial assistance include the following:

Scholarships
Many colleges offer scholarships to talented students in a variety of fields such as athletics, Reserve Officer Training Corps (ROTC), academics, and the arts. Scholarships are usually small but need not be repaid.

Grants
The Pell Grant, named for the legislator who sponsored the bill, is an example of a federal program that provides financial assistance to students. This type of grant is made to students who demonstrate financial need and document the need through the Free Application for Federal Financial Aid. These grants range from $400 to $2,700.

Additional grants are available through the following sources (contact your counselor for details):

- (your state) Higher Education Grant
- Pennsylvania Higher Education Assistance Agency
- Shaw Scholarship
- Bureau of Indian Affairs
- National Achievement Scholarship Program for outstanding African-American students
- National Merit Scholarships
- Veterans Educational Benefits
- Vocational Rehabilitation (students with specific handicaps)
- Many colleges operate their own or state-supported financial assistance programs. College catalogs normally include this type of information.

Loans

Numerous loan programs are also available, based on financial eligibility. Some examples include:

- William D. Ford Federal Direct Loan. If eligible, $2625 may be borrowed for your freshman year, $3500 for the sophomore year, and $5500 per year for the junior and senior years. Repayment begins six months after graduation or when you cease to be a full-time student.
- Federal Direct Parent Loan for Undergraduate Students. Parents of dependent students may apply for loans up to the cost of education, less other aid awarded. The interest rate is adjusted annually but is capped at 9 percent.

These loans must be repaid. Interest is charged beginning after graduation. Local banks also offer a variety of loan programs, with rates geared to the economy at the time the loan is granted. Also check on the availability of state-sponsored, benefactor-sponsored, and other loans at your college.

Work-Study Programs

Work-study programs are federal- and state-supported programs that give students the opportunity to earn money while gaining practical work experience. Placement offices at a college or university attempt to put students in jobs related to their field of study. You may also consider working part-time during the school year and the summers to finance part of your educational expenses.

Teacher Scholarships
During periods of teacher shortage, particularly in areas such as special education, science, and mathematics, some of the states offer financial aid to encourage students to enter these fields. Recipients of financial aid must promise to teach in the state for a specified time following graduation.

Aid from the Military
For those who wish to delay college until they complete service in the military, financial help is provided. Consult your local recruiting officer for details.

WHAT ARE THE COLLEGE REQUIREMENTS FOR BECOMING A TEACHER?

Once you have decided to become a teacher and have selected a college, you must decide on a major and minor teaching field. That decision is discussed in the latter part of this chapter. Regardless of your major or minor, however, the structure of your educational program is very similar.

The first two years of college provide a broad base in the arts, humanities, English, and other languages. Programs vary in the number and timing of the electives offered. Some teacher-training programs do not have supervised practice or any practical experience until the senior year. Others integrate practical experience throughout the four years. With the assistance of your college adviser, you select the courses you take.

A typical college operating on a semester basis requires at least 120 to 128 hours of college credit for a bachelor's degree. A course may carry one to three or more semester credits. Your courses will change each semester. A sample schedule for prospective teachers can be broken into four categories of courses:

1. Basic courses (eleven credit hours minimum). All students must take basic courses in English, mathematics, and physical education in order to graduate. These are normally taken as part of the first thirty hours.

2. Liberal arts courses (twenty-nine credit hours minimum). Courses in the fine arts, humanities (such as history, philosophy, or literature), natural sciences, and social sciences count toward liberal arts requirements. These courses should be taken as part of the first ninety hours.

3. Professional education courses (twelve to fifteen credit hours minimum). These courses build the foundations of educational training. They include teaching laboratories and internships where students are placed with a trained supervising teacher to gain actual experience in conducting classes on a daily basis.

4. Courses that fulfill the requirements for a major and minor subject (thirty to sixty hours). Major and minor subjects will be discussed in depth later in this chapter.

The courses you study are designed to give you a common core of information and to help you to become a well-rounded person while pursuing your interests. In addition to the courses listed, electives are interspersed in the program to balance your interests and prevent scheduling conflicts.

HOW SHOULD YOU CHOOSE MAJOR AND MINOR FIELDS OF SPECIALIZATION?

Your major is the area of study in which you will become an expert. It requires more courses, more time, more work, and more attention to getting good grades than other subjects, but it will pay greater dividends in the future.

Depending on the school and the subject area you have chosen, your major will require between thirty and sixty semester hours of credit. Many colleges and universities have increased subject requirements as well. Some schools offer a double major, meaning that you graduate with qualifications in two major fields of specialization.

As a preliminary step in choosing your major field, consider the following questions:

- In which subject areas have I done my best work? Are these the areas that I would like to pursue in college?
- Do I have special talents that will guide my choice of specialization?
- Have my hobbies or my extracurricular activities given me any further insight into my real areas of interest?
- Am I interested in one or more of the areas in which there is a predicted shortage of teachers?
- Do I prefer working with younger children, adolescents, or older students?
- If I am still undecided, will I be able to change my major field at the end of my freshman or sophomore year?

You need to make a choice of the grade levels or subject area for your major. The options that are open to you include the following:

Elementary School
If you are leaning toward the choice of teaching in elementary school, your major should aim toward one of the following areas (keeping in mind, however, that some schools will require you to major in a subject area):

1. Preschool. Some schools offer programs geared toward children from three to five years of age. Some of these programs are custodial in nature, taking care of children of working parents. Others include readiness activities to prepare children for academic work. Some special education programs include work with children younger than three.
2. Kindergarten. This is normally the grade before first grade.
3. Primary grades. In most elementary schools, the grades included are one through three.
4. Intermediate grades. Except in schools that feed into a middle school, the grades included are four through six. Schools associated with a middle school normally include grades four and five. (Some schools are organized with kindergarten through grade seven or grade eight.)

Most elementary school teachers teach all academic subjects. Other specialists on the staff may cover many of the following:

- Remedial reading
- Physical education
- Special education
- Vocal music

- Art
- Foreign languages
- Guidance counselor
- School nurse
- Instrumental music
- Speech and hearing
- Librarian or media center librarian
- School psychologist

Secondary School

If you choose to work toward teaching in a middle school, junior high school, or high school, your major will definitely focus on a subject field. Courses will vary, depending on the size of the school and the budget of the school district, but your major will be in one of the following areas:

1. English: literature, grammar, composition, journalism, speech, and drama
2. Social sciences: various courses in history, geography, sociology, and economics
3. Mathematics: applied math and business math, algebra, geometry, trigonometry, calculus, computer math, analysis and probability
4. Science: general science, biology, chemistry, physics, physical science, earth science, microbiology, physiology, geology, and medical science
5. Career education: courses in business education, home economics, industrial arts, and trade-oriented skills
6. Physical education
7. Music: vocal and instrumental
8. Health education
9. Art
10. Foreign languages
11. Special education

Numerous support staff members are assigned to secondary schools, including the following:

- Media center librarian
- School nurse
- School psychologist
- Computer coordinator
- College placement counselor
- Security counselor
- Guidance counselor

Minor Field of Specialization

The minor field does not usually require as many credits as the major. Most colleges require between eighteen and twenty-four credit hours. Many now require that the minor be in a subject area. As mentioned earlier, some schools offer a double major instead of a minor, to give additional emphasis to scholarship and subject specialization.

A minor or double major offers an added option, both when you are seeking a position and when you are given teaching assignments by your principal. It can mean job security during times of staff cutbacks. Also, a minor can become a major interest at some time in the future.

SETTING SHORT-RANGE AND LONG-RANGE GOALS

After you have chosen your major and minor, you should consider setting both short-term and long-term goals. The game of football is a good example of these types of goals. The overall strategy of the game is to score touchdowns, but individual plays are designed to achieve the short-term goal, the first down. Your immediate *short-range goals* might include the following:

- Get good grades during the first semester of my freshman year
- Prove to my parents that I can do well in the college I have chosen
- Find out if I have chosen a program that really interests me

Your *long-range goals* might be to:

- Earn at least a 3.0 grade point average during four years of college
- Graduate in the upper quarter of my class
- Find a teaching position in the location of my choice
- Plan for a minimum of a master's degree

If your goals are not yet clearly defined, and if you still have doubts about whether you have made the right career choice, you are not alone. Most students have the same doubts, and it is the rare person who does not make course changes, changes in a major or minor, and even career changes. In fact, it is estimated that most people make a minimum of three changes during their working careers.

4

Getting a Professional License and Certification

Have you ever noticed the many diplomas and certificates displayed in the offices of doctors, barbers, dentists, optometrists, and lawyers? The diplomas serve two purposes. The first is to recognize that the professional completed an approved program or course of study and has demonstrated an ability to be successful in that field. The second purpose is to assure the client or patient that the professional person has met these requirements and that trust can be placed in his or her work.

PROFESSIONAL LICENSURE AND CERTIFICATION

Why is this necessary? The state and the profession have an interest in seeing that only competent professionals practice in the state and the nation. When you hire a lawyer, consult a doctor, or even get a haircut, the person providing the service will possess some type of state license to do business in that state. If standards were not established, particularly for entry-level performance, the public would have to rely on trial and error methods of finding professional help.

Licensure, or the teaching license, is the permit granted by the state department of education or state standards board to a teacher to practice in the state. Certification is a voluntary advanced process of teacher recognition by a self-governing board with a majority of teachers. However, many state departments and even teachers refer to a state license as teacher certification. This is still acceptable for a short period of time.

STATE LICENSURE

Once you have a college diploma in hand, you must be licensed in the state in which you wish to teach. If you want to teach in the state where you attended college and you completed an approved teacher education program, you will need only apply to the state department or state standards board with your credentials. Often, licensure is also completed as part of your teacher training program.

In general, state licensure requirements include a bachelor's degree from an approved college or university, education-related experience such as student teaching, courses specifically related to the region or state, and the passing of a national or state test.

If you wish to teach in another state, you must have your college record sent to that state's department of education or board of teaching. That department will evaluate your credentials and inform you of any requirements you need to complete before receiving a license.

Since you did not complete an approved program for that state, your credentials will probably be reviewed through a process called course review. Your individual courses and experiences will be compared to that state's requirements to determine whether you are eligible for a license. This is not an exact process; it takes time and can be appealed. If you lack certain requirements for that particular state license, you may still be hired by a local school board, but you must complete those requirements as soon as possible to earn your license and to retain your position. Some states have worked out reciprocity agreements with neighboring states under which each state accepts the other state's graduates.

The current lack of a completely operational system of teacher self-governance and the increased public concern for teacher and educational quality has led many states to institute teacher competency testing programs for licensure in addition to the other generally acceptable assessment programs such as the National Teacher Examination requirement. Teacher licensure requirements in a particular state may include:

- Bachelor's degree from an accredited college of teacher education
- Successful student teaching experience
- Acceptable scores on related portions of the National Teacher Examination (acceptable scores set by each state)
- Recommendations from other members of the profession
- State-administered tests of professional competency

Currently more than thirty-five states administer some portion of the National Teacher Examination (NTE) to licensure candidates. The NTE is a paper-and-pencil test covering subject areas and pedagogy (teaching practice). It is administered by the

Educational Testing Service (ETS) in Princeton, New Jersey. The ETS has launched a revised assessment system for teacher licensure, which it hopes will be adopted by states over a five-year period to replace the NTE. This system, titled Praxis: Professional Assessments for Beginning Teachers, offers state-of-the-art advances in teacher assessment methods.

TEACHING STANDARDS

The increasing concern for the quality of teachers has led individual states to establish acceptable standards for beginning teachers and to establish methods, usually tests, to measure whether beginning teacher candidates possess these standards. Some states are requiring currently employed teachers to pass "master teacher" tests in order to renew their teaching licenses.

This process of establishing teaching standards and measurements has encountered many difficulties and much expense for individual states; as a result, many states are cooperating on establishing consistent standards and methods of assessment. One example is the Interstate New Teachers Assessment and Support Consortium operated by the Council of Chief State School Officers in Washington, DC. This group has developed a set of standards for new teachers and is encouraging states to use them for initial licensure. Those standards include the following.

A teacher:
- Understands central concepts, structures, and tools of inquiry of discipline(s)
- Understands how children learn and develop and provides opportunities for intellectual, social, and personal development

- Understands how students differ and creates opportunities for diverse learners
- Understands and uses a variety of instructional techniques for problem solving, higher-order thinking skills, and performance
- Understands individual and group motivation to create learning environments for positive interaction and engagement in learning
- Understands verbal and nonverbal communication to foster collaboration and interaction
- Plans instruction on knowledge of discipline, students, community, and curriculum
- Understands formal and informal assessment procedures to foster learning
- Fosters relationships with colleagues, parents, and community to support learning

PERFORMANCE-BASED REQUIREMENTS

If you look closely at the standards above, you will realize that it would be very difficult to test some of these items with a paper-and-pencil test. Observation by other professionals, collection of portfolios, and other methods must be used to assess these standards. Many states have begun to establish experience- or performance-based requirements in addition to student teaching for a new teacher to receive a license. For example, a teacher might spend his or her first year in a probationary placement with a mentor teacher or evaluator in order to demonstrate his or her ability to maintain the standards. A beginning teacher who successfully completes a probationary period may be moved on to the next probationary phase, which may extend for two to three years. During this phase the

39

new teacher will continue to meet the daily performance requirements for successful teaching through school and district evaluations. The next phase includes a continuing contract with the district and a state teaching license. The final phase begins when a licensed teacher decides to become a mentor to other new teachers as a lead teacher.

TEACHING CERTIFICATES

Teaching licenses (certificates) vary by state, but usually fall into the following patterns. The first type of license is a provisional license, which allows you to teach for one to seven years depending upon state regulations, until you complete the requirements of a professional certificate. The professional certificate usually must be renewed every three to five years by a continuing education requirement, such as taking additional college courses or earning approved in-service credit.

After completing a master's degree or a set number of renewals, you receive a permanent professional certificate, which does not need to be renewed in that state for the remainder of your career. If you change states, the licensure process begins again but is simplified by your advanced training and degrees, successful experience, and potential licensure reciprocity agreements among states.

CERTIFICATE REVOCATION

The teacher licensure and certification system also has continuing responsibilities for teachers. A license or certificate can be revoked by the awarding agency (the state) upon recommendation from the local school district for various reasons. The reasons can include incompetence, immorality, insubordination, or failure to perform duties. Revocation of a license is rare.

ALTERNATIVE CERTIFICATION

Teachers who undergo alternative certification are usually hired to fill a teacher shortage in a particular area such as mathematics, physics, or bilingual education. They usually have a demonstrated interest and ability to teach, have a college degree, and have agreed to work toward a license by completing education-related courses and training. They receive lower pay and have less job security than other teachers as long as they have alternative status.

TEACHER EVALUATION

If you are a practicing teacher, even with a permanent license, your teaching competency will be evaluated. Your school principal or an instructional supervisor will be responsible for assessing your continued performance, usually through observation of your teaching throughout the year. If your skills need improvement, workshops, training, and conferences may be provided for you under the title of in-service or staff development. Local and state school districts have a responsibility to offer continued training opportunities for teachers. Local school systems often offer a series of training opportunities for all teachers for continued growth.

ADVANCED DEGREES

Three basic college degrees are of benefit to you in teaching. The first is the bachelor's degree. The bachelor of arts (B.A.) or bachelor of science (B.S.) with a concentration in education is a four-year undergraduate degree in education and is considered the minimum requirement for licensure and certification in the teaching field. The second is the master of arts (M.A.) or master of science (M.S.), which takes approximately one year of full-time graduate study or several years of part-time study. This degree often is the highest one that school teachers need because it carries permanent licensure and certification in most states. The doctor of philosophy (Ph.D.) or doctor of education (Ed.D.) is a graduate degree usually earned over three to five years, with one year in full-time residence. It is obtained by people interested in teaching at the college level, doing research, or working toward higher-level positions in administration.

Salary Schedule

The more degrees or training you have, the higher salary you are likely to receive. Some systems provide a pay increase for each fifteen semester hours successfully completed. Of course, you must weigh the cost of courses against the salary increase. In the short run, you may lose money on advanced training if your coursework is not paid for by the school system, but over the long run you will earn more money with advanced degrees. Remember, you may be teaching for thirty or more years before retirement.

Self-Confidence and Status

Another reason for obtaining advanced training is to increase your self-confidence by becoming more certain and proficient in teaching your subject area. With this confidence you will be a better teacher and be more respected among students and colleagues.

Master's Degree Before Beginning Teaching
Should you obtain a master's degree before your first year of teaching? Naturally, the answer depends on your aspirations, your finances, the requirements of your field, and the competition for jobs in your subject area. Our recommendations are as follows.

Do not get your master's degree before your first year of teaching if that experience is to be in elementary or secondary teaching. First, you will be more competitive in the job market if you have only a bachelor's degree. How can that be? A teacher with a bachelor's degree earn less than a teacher with a master's degree; if a school system is looking at the budget closely, hiring new teachers at the bottom of the scale can save money.

Second, advanced training in teaching will be more meaningful to you after you have had some experience. Third, a part-time approach can save you money and increase your options for additional experience. If possible, obtain each of your degrees from a different institution to further broaden your exposure to ideas and experiences.

Beginning Your Career in Teaching

Your first teaching position is very special, since it will set the stage for your success as a teacher and for the positions that follow. For this reason, you should give careful consideration to the following questions as part of your personal job application procedure:

- Where do you want to teach?
- What type of position do you really want?
- Should you teach in a public school or a private school?
- Should you consider a teaching position in another country?
- Are other types of positions available in the United States?
- What position appears to offer the best future?

WHERE CAN YOU TEACH?

Many of the factors in deciding where you want to teach are personal, but all of the questions are important in making your choice of the specific area. You need to face the following questions squarely, since they will have a major impact on your job satisfaction and future happiness:

- Other than going to college, have you lived away from home before, so that homesickness will not be a problem?
- Do you have compelling reasons for wanting to be located near your current home?
- How far from home are you willing to move to find a suitable position?
- Do you have financial obligations that make it necessary for you to live with your parents?
- Are you married? Does your spouse work in the same or another profession? Do you have children to consider in the decision?
- Would you have to own a good car for long commutes?
- Is suitable and affordable housing available?
- Do politics enter into the selection and placement of teachers in the community?
- Does the school or school system have a good reputation?
- Does the community show respect for its teachers and schools, and does the budget reflect this high level of support?

If you are a highly qualified teacher and if you meet the licensure and certification requirements for the school or school system, you should be able to begin your career either in a small community or in a metropolitan area, and also in a school of the size you prefer.

What Type of Position Do You Desire?

If your major is elementary education, do you want to teach kindergarten, grade three, or grade six? If grade six is your choice, do you want to teach in a school that has self-contained classes, or would you prefer a departmentalized organization? Administrative organizations for elementary schools include:

Team Teaching

Two or more teachers working together, with a larger number of students. Each team member is responsible for teaching his or her subject to the entire group of students.

Classes for Exceptional Students

Some schools are organized entirely for talented and gifted (TAG) classes; some are organized for students with learning difficulties; and others offer this type of program in addition to regular classes.

Traditional Self-Contained School

This organizational type refers to a separate classroom with a teacher and students assigned to a room for a particular grade or level of instruction. This school usually values strict discipline, a dress code, generous homework assignments, and emphasis on the academic subject areas.

Open School

Students are allowed to move from group to group, learning at their own pace and, often, according to their own interests. The open school may operate in a building with movable walls and large amounts of open space.

Focus School

As part of a desegregation plan, parents are given a choice of the type of school program they want for their children. Some specialized schools offer concentrations on particular subjects such as the performing arts while also teaching the traditional subjects. Others might include foreign language studies or classes for the talented and gifted, using some of the organizational patterns described above.

In choosing an elementary school position, you might also consider whether the school staff includes aides to assist you with clerical duties, aides to monitor the cafeteria during the lunch period, and special teachers for subjects such as music, physical education, art, library skills, and remedial reading. Are there also specialists in speech, guidance, and special education? What nonteaching duties are assigned to teachers?

For your own personal growth, is the principal a leader who can help you to improve your teaching skills, and is additional supervisory assistance available? Are teachers involved in decision-making at the school level? Are adequate resources available to teachers?

If you plan to teach in a secondary school, you need to be concerned about the administrative organization of the school as you choose the type of assignment you hope to receive. Your major and minor fields of specialization make you eligible to teach your subject or subjects in a middle school, a junior high school, or a high school, so you need to decide what age level of students you really like to work with. The age level makes a difference in how you use your subject-matter expertise. If, for example, you are a math major, would you prefer teaching general math to slower-learning and, perhaps, hard-to-motivate junior high students; do you hope to have a teaching load that includes students at all ability levels; or are you interested only in teaching high-level courses to college-bound students?

Your teaching assignment could include two subjects, so your minor field of specialization is also important. If you are qualified in both English and social studies, your assignment could include classes in both subjects.

Many secondary schools follow specialized administrative organizational patterns, including:

Magnet School
Specialized school for students in subjects such as the visual and performing arts—music, dance, art, and theater—or science and technology.

Vocational-Technical Center
School that offers training for a specific trade such as carpentry, air conditioning, welding, automobile repair, electronics, or cosmetology.

Science and Technology Center
School that offers courses in higher mathematics, preengineering technology, advanced science, and technology.

Alternative School
School, sometimes called a "last-chance" school, that offers programs for disruptive or dropout-prone students.

Open School
Program similar to the elementary school model, but offering courses and studies at the high school level.

Comprehensive High School
This is the more common secondary school pattern in the country. All services and programs for all students are offered on the same campus.

In addition to knowing the organizational pattern and size of the school, you also need to know your teaching load. How many periods will you teach, what is the average size of classes, how much will you need to prepare for each day, and what will be your total student load?

Other considerations include whether the school is organized on a six-period or seven-period day, the number of free or planning periods in your schedule, what nonteaching duties you will be assigned, and whether you will have clerical assistance. The leadership skills of the department chairperson, principal, and assistant principals are important considerations, as well as the type and quality of supervision that is available.

Should You Teach in a Public School or a Private School?

Since more than 80 percent of the available teaching positions are in public schools, it seems obvious that you have a greater chance of getting the type of teaching position you want in a public school. Public schools are governed by a local or district board of education, which establishes the conditions of employment. Each local board—there are more than 14,000 in the United States—must meet standards established by the state department of education or the state legislature. Since state financial structures and ability to pay for education differ, there is a wide variation in teaching conditions among the fifty states and within any one state.

Private schools have even more differences in teaching conditions. These schools have been established for a variety of reasons, including the desire of parents for religious training in the course of studies, military-type discipline, a college preparatory curriculum, specialized help for learning disabilities, or a school away from the home environment for their children. Many private schools offer salaries equal to or better than those of the public schools. Other private schools operate on restricted budgets, and the teacher pay reflects the lack of finances. Whether you are considering a position with a public or private school, you need to check the conditions of employment with care. A good question to ask yourself is whether the position could be a career position. Also, if you are leaning toward a private school position, check whether you need to be certified and whether accreditation of the school is a state requirement.

Should You Consider a Teaching Position in Another Country?

There are thousands of teaching positions in American schools located in foreign countries. These assignments usually are not considered career positions, since most of the contracts are for periods of from one to three years. If you are interested in a job that gives you the satisfaction of teaching and at the same time allows you to see other areas of the world, you should investigate this type of opportunity. Check the experience requirements, however, since many overseas schools have an age minimum and require applicants to have several years of teaching experience. Some schools also require a master's degree. This may be an opportunity to consider at a later point in your career.

If you are married, another consideration might be whether the school would allow family members to accompany you. Most of the overseas assignments are available in the following types of programs:

International schools
- U.S. Army, Navy, and Air Force Schools for Dependent Children
- Schools operated by corporations for children of employees
- Schools in U.S. territories and possessions
- Exchange Teacher Programs
- Private schools in other countries
- University of Maryland overseas undergraduate program and other programs sponsored by American universities.

Other Positions Available in the United States

A number of teaching positions are available, many of them through federal and state agencies. These assignments are interesting and challenging because of the location and the type of students served. Among them are:

- Schools on military bases to serve dependent children of personnel assigned to the installation.
- Detention homes, training schools, and reformatories to serve students who have been committed to the institution by the courts. Most of these schools are supported and operated by the state.
- Laboratory schools in colleges and universities that offer teacher training. These schools serve several purposes, including training teachers (through student teaching experiences), testing experimental programs, and teaching the students who have enrolled. Positions in these schools often carry the rank and status of college instructor.
- Schools for Native American children. These schools are located throughout the United States,

including Alaska, Arizona, California, Colorado, Florida, Montana, Oklahoma, and Wyoming.
- Programs such as Teach for America, which place college graduates (of any major) in underfunded school districts, either in rural or urban areas.

What Position Appears to Offer the Best Future?

The director of personnel of a large metropolitan school system often asked teacher applicants, "Where do you see yourself five years from now?" After hearing the reply, he would counter with, "What about ten years?" As you think about where you want to teach and the type of position you hope to get, you might also consider whether that position appears to offer the type of experience that will help you to prepare for future positions.

Answers to the following questions could help you to determine whether a specific position appears to offer the best future:

- Is the school within commuting distance of a college or university that offers a program for continuing work toward advanced degrees?
- Is the school system large enough to offer opportunities for advancement, in the event that you decide to seek an administrative or supervisory position?
- Does the school system offer a sabbatical leave to enable you to continue your research or complete your graduate studies?
- Does the salary scale include a career level, making it possible for you to continue to teach, if that is your long-term goal?

How Do You Obtain Your First Position?

In many respects, your job search will involve a process similar to that of choosing your college or university. After you have decided on the area in which you hope to teach and the type of position you want, your job search depends on several factors:

- Is there a teacher shortage in the school system? Are many positions available in the school or school system that you have selected as your first choice?
- Does the school system use recruiting teams to find qualified teacher applicants?
- Does the system offer incentives to attract teachers?
- Are you fully qualified for the position you seek?
- Are you fully certified?
- Do you have a master's degree or have you taken courses beyond the bachelor's degree?
- Do your major and minor fields of specialization match the teaching position you are seeking?
- Do you have average or better recommendations from your student teaching or practice teaching experience?
- Are your college grades high enough to convince a prospective employer that you are well grounded in subject matter and teaching techniques?
- Do you have confidence in yourself?
- Are you convinced that you are prepared to begin your teaching career? Can you sell yourself to the personnel officer?

If There Is a Teacher Shortage

If you are applying for a teaching position in a school system that is experiencing a shortage of qualified applicants, you can be more selective in finding the position of your choice. It is also possible that the school system will use special recruiters to identify the most promising prospects among the current college or university graduates. The recruiters may come to your campus.

If a recruiter visits your campus, information will be available in the placement office, which will assign the recruiter a temporary office and set up a schedule of appointments for applicants. The recruiter will supply you with a brochure describing the school system and its communities, an application form, and information to answer your personal questions. Whether or not you have the advantage of meeting with a recruiter, you will probably have to take the following steps as part of the application procedure:

- Complete the application form for the school system.
- Provide an official transcript of your college or university work.
- Visit the central office of the school system for an interview in the personnel department. (An interview with a recruiter might satisfy this requirement.)
- Take a written test administered by the personnel department. Some tests are national standardized tests; others are designed to fit the needs of the local school system. Most of the tests are geared to screen out candidates who are weak in mathematics, spelling, grammar, or composition.

Make sure that your résumé is complete and up to date. You will want to give a copy to a recruiter or the personnel officer with whom you meet. Even if teachers are in short supply, you should visit the school system in person to get as much first-hand information as possible. This information will be invaluable in helping you decide if the position is one you really want.

If Teaching Positions Are Difficult to Find

If teaching positions are scarce in the area and school system of your choice, most of the initiative in the job search will be up to you. You will need to use some additional steps to determine whether positions are available and to seek information on specific application procedures. Most graduates use the following procedures in seeking their first teaching positions.

Visit your school's placement office.

The placement office is in contact with the personnel departments of most of the school systems in the area served by that college or university. Information should also be available on positions in private schools, colleges, and overseas schools. A visit to the placement office can help you find possible vacancies and the office or person to approach concerning teaching positions. Many of the larger school districts have recorded telephone messages listing available jobs.

Write a letter to the superintendent or director of personnel.

Write to the appropriate person, by name, to indicate your interest in a teaching position. The letter should be brief and to the point, but should include all pertinent questions. A typed letter is preferable, and be sure your spelling, grammar, and punctuation are correct. The accompanying letter can be used as a guide.

9050 Maple Street
Frosttown, Maryland 20510
Date

Dr. Hal Winstanding
Superintendent of Schools
Cumberland Township
Allegany, Maryland 20500

Dear Dr. Winstanding:

I am interested in obtaining a teaching position in the Cumberland Township School System and would like to request information on the procedure for submitting an application.

My papers are on file with the placement office of the Frosttown State College, and I will graduate this May with a major in mathematics and a minor in science. A résumé summarizing my activities and experience is enclosed. My goal is to begin my teaching career in a junior high school.

If the Township has published a brochure describing the school system and conditions of employment, please send one to me, along with an application form.

I will be available for an interview during the spring break in March or after graduation in May.

Thank you for your consideration of my requests.

Sincerely yours,

Yolanda Smith

When you have received the information from the school system, complete the application form accurately and neatly and mail it back to the appropriate officer. If you did not send a résumé with your letter of inquiry, enclose a copy with the application form. If a short written essay is called for, be sure it is done neatly and in correct form.

Develop a résumé.
Although the use of a standardized application form makes the résumé unnecessary for many school systems, you should still consider developing your own biographical outline for enclosure with your letter of inquiry.

A good test for a résumé is to make certain that it contains the following elements:

- It is completely accurate.
- It covers all of the major categories that you want to highlight for a prospective employer.
- It contains only pertinent information.
- It is set up in an attractive format.
- It relates specifically to the position for which you are applying.
- It is individually typed or reproduced by a process that makes it look like an original.
- It contains a recent photograph similar to a passport photo (optional).

The following sample résumé may be helpful to you in the preparation of your biographical data:

Yolanda Smith
9050 Maple Street
Frosttown, Maryland 20510

POSITION GOAL: Junior high mathematics teacher

EDUCATION
Frosttown State College—B.S. in Education, 1997,
    major in mathematics, minor in science
University of Maryland—six hours in concurrent
    enrollment program for high school honors
    students

TEACHING EXPERIENCE
Student teaching (nine weeks) in college lab school
Student teaching (nine weeks) in Western Junior
    High School
Substitute teacher (total of four weeks) in
    Cumberland Township Junior High School

PROFESSIONAL ORGANIZATIONS
Student National Education Association member

HONORS
Phi Delta Kappa

AUTHOR
"Developing a Field Trip Guide for Junior High
    School," *Science Quarterly*, Vol. III, September
    1997.

EXTRACURRICULAR ACTIVITIES
Varsity volleyball (two years)
Member, Science Club (three years)

Gather firsthand information on the school and school system.
Graduates of your college or university can be excellent sources of information, and you should take advantage of their insights. However, one or more personal visits to the school under consideration are essential if you hope to make a wise decision on your first teaching assignment.

Prepare for your interview.
Most employers regard the interview as crucial in determining whether to offer the applicant a contract. Your goals are to make a favorable impression and to convince the employer that you are the best person for the position. Be sure to dress appropriately and be prepared to answer a variety of questions.

Be yourself. Answer the questions straightforwardly, and do not be afraid to say, "I don't know," rather than trying to bluff an answer. Personnel officers have had a lot of experience and can easily spot a phony answer.

A good technique in preparing for the interview is to pretend that you are the interviewer. What questions would you want to ask a candidate for the position you are seeking? They would probably include:

- Why are you interested in this particular position?
- What experience have you had that makes you think you could be a successful teacher in this community?
- What nonteaching experience do you think will be helpful to you?
- Describe your approach to disciplinary problems.
- What position do you hope to hold at the end of five years? Ten years?

The interview also gives you an opportunity to ask questions and clarify your impressions of the school or school system. As a beginning teacher, you should make certain that you have accurate information concerning:

- The community in which the school is located
- The exact location of the school
- Appropriate housing
- The school calendar
- Pay and fringe benefits
- Cost of living
- Recertification requirements
- Supervision
- Class size
- Extra duties
- Size of school
- Location of colleges with graduate programs
- Other personal and professional opportunities
- The school staff
- Decision-making philosophy for the schools and the system

Take a written test.
In response to public criticism that some teachers are unprepared in basic skill areas, many school systems now use a written test to screen out teachers who lack skills in writing, spelling, grammar, and mathematics. In most instances, these tests are given on the same day as the interview and are scored right away, so that the personnel department and the applicant can have almost immediate feedback. If you are a good student, you probably need not prepare for this test. However, if

you have trouble with the fundamentals, you may want to do some serious review work. Some school systems realize that certain people get nervous in testing situations, and they allow applicants to take the test again after a waiting period of one month.

Decide whether you will use an agency
Some people like to work with a teacher-placement agency in the search for their first teaching assignment. If you are leaning in that direction, be sure to choose an agency with a good track record of placement. You should be certain that your personnel records are up to date and accurate and that they include all the required documents, which will probably include:

- Letters of recommendation
- Your résumé
- Copies of your college transcripts
- Photographs (if required)

See if your college placement office offers the service of maintaining and updating your personnel files. This can be of tremendous help down the road in your career.

Before you sign a contract with an agency, read all the fine print.
You need to know the length of the contract, the cost, and whether the agency is working directly for you, as opposed to sending several candidates for an advertised opening. Many teaching contracts are for one year, and the agency normally charges you a percentage of your first year's salary if you get a position as a result of its service.

Before Signing Your Contract
If you have found a teaching position that you consider ideal and have received an official job offer and a contract to be signed, you need to pause and reflect on the following questions:

- Are the terms of the contract acceptable?
- Is it the position you really want?
- Is the contract an "open contract," or does it specify the exact position on which you have agreed?
- Will you be represented by a collective bargaining agreement?
- Is the beginning salary acceptable?
- Is the salary scale a "career scale" (one that rewards those who elect to remain in the classroom during their entire teaching career)?
- Are there satisfactory fringe benefits to complement the salary?
- Is the probationary period both fair and acceptable?
- When will you be offered tenure?
- Are there any unsatisfactory conditions associated with the position?
- Will you have the type of supervision, back-up support, and materials of instruction that will assist you with steady professional growth?

After Signing Your Contract
When you have signed and returned the contract to your new employer, you should have a sense of excitement and anticipation. Most beginning teachers find it helpful to visit their new schools before the end of the school year, to see them in action, while the students

are there. The visit can be arranged by getting in touch with the principal, and it will give you a chance to begin your professional relationship with your new boss.

You should be able to get into your classroom either during the summer or just before the start of the school year. As a beginning teacher, you will want to study the curriculum, review the textbooks and reference materials, check on the availability of computers and audiovisual aids, and meet staff members with whom you will be working. You may be assigned a "buddy teacher" to help with your orientation as well as be expected to attend a formal induction program. In short, there are dozens of things you need to do to get ready for that day when your students arrive.

As a beginning teacher you will be in a position both to lead and to learn. The experienced teachers will watch you, not only to see how you are doing, but to find out what new ideas you have brought from your college or university experience. You can expect to be "tested" by your students to find out what type of disciplinarian you are and how well you teach them.

How Much Will You Earn As a Teacher?

A common belief is that teaching is one of the least rewarding and lower paying of the professions. This belief has affected the quantity and quality of persons entering schools of education in recent years. Currently, however, many steps have been taken to correct years of neglect by policy makers. Salaries are becoming competitive once again and, combined with fringe benefits, make a teaching career a very attractive prospect for a young person to consider.

Intangible Rewards

If you talk to most experienced teachers who have made a career of teaching, you will find that they had more than monetary reasons for choosing a teaching career. The profession that you choose affects the style of life that you will lead for twenty to forty years. Anyone will tell you that money alone cannot buy happiness in a career of that many years. Teaching is a profession that offers its share of personal satisfaction. The excitement of seeing a student excel in school and become a success in life is rewarding. Equally rewarding is helping someone who is having trouble with reading, writing, or science to become a good student. To make an enlightened career choice, both tangible and intangible rewards must be weighed into the decision.

Whether you teach in public or private school, or college, your salary is based on schedules. Individual salaries are negotiated as in many other kinds of work. Negotiations are within the schedules for the total group. The salary schedules may be based upon a state salary minimum or, in some cases, based upon conditions within the district. For each year of experience you gain, your salary moves up the schedule. In addition, advanced degrees increase your salary. Salaries are adjusted frequently to take into account inflation, increased revenues from taxes, union negotiations, and other factors. Salary schedules tend to treat excellent teachers the same as average teachers; however, they do promote fairness and establish a standard for the profession. Later in this chapter, the issue of merit pay for excellent teachers is discussed.

Salary schedules are established by the state or county government, depending on the state in which you teach. Thus salaries can vary from one school district to another and from state to state. Private school salaries usually are competitive with public school teacher salaries in the same geographical area. The salary schedules on p. 69 are provided to illustrate various types of schedules that you may encounter.

Fringe Benefits

As public employees, public school teachers receive fringe benefits that are among the best in the professions. They range from items such as health insurance, holidays, and vacation schedules to retirement plans. Fringe benefits can have either immediate use, such as sick days, or long-range use, such as retirement investments. Sample benefits are discussed below.

Tenure

In most school systems, tenure is a fringe benefit. As a beginning teacher, you must work from one to three years as a probationary teacher. During this time, you are supervised by your principal, district supervisor, or others. The purpose of probation is much like an internship for doctors, to ensure quality within the profession. Once you have demonstrated your competence as a teacher, you are granted tenure. That means you cannot be dismissed or demoted unless you violate certain legal rules, usually willful neglect of duty, incompetence, immorality, dishonesty, insubordination, or intemperance. Your employment with that system is indefinite, instead of year to year. However, if you change districts you often lose tenure and must prove yourself again.

65

AVERAGE SALARIES BY STATE

1. Alabama	32,799	26. Missouri	34,001
2. Alaska	48,275	27. Montana	30,617
3 Arizona	34,071	28. Nebraska	32,668
4. Arkansas	32,119	29. Nevada	40,572
5. California	44,585	30. New Hampshire	36,633
6. Colorado	37,240	31. New Jersey	50,284
7. Connecticut	51,727	32. New York	48,712
8. Delaware	42,439	33. New Mexico	30,309
9. District of	44,746	34. North Carolina	33,123
Columbia		35. North Dakota	28,231
10. Florida	34,473	36. Ohio	39,099
11. Georgia	37,410	37. Oklahoma	30,940
12. Hawaii	36,598	38. Oregon	42,301
13. Idaho	32,834	39. Pennsylvania	47,543
14. Illinois	43,707	40. Rhode Island	44,506
15. Indiana	39,752	41. South Carolina	33,608
16. Iowa	34,084	42 South Dakota	27,839
17. Kansas	33,800	43. Tennessee	34,584
18. Kentucky	34,453	44. Texas	33,537
19. Louisiana	30,090	45. Utah	32,981
20. Maine	34,349	46. Vermont	36,299
21. Maryland	41,404	47. Virginia	37,024
22. Massachusetts	44,285	48. Washington	38,755
23. Michigan	48,361	49. Wisconsin	38,179
24. Minnesota	39,104	50. West Virginia	33,396
25. Mississippi	28,691	51. Wyoming	32,022

Sample salary schedules. Comparisons are often made about the discrepancies among salaries in teaching and other professions such as medicine, law, or dentistry. One cause of the difference is that teaching in public schools is regulated by agencies of state and local government. As a public school teacher you are a public employee who is paid with tax funds.

SAMPLE SALARY SCHEDULE I

Years	Provisional Certificate (Bachelor's)	Standard Certificate (Master's)	Advanced Certificate (Master's Plus)
1	31,000	32,800	
2	31,650	33,300	
3	32,300	33,950	
4	32,950	34,600	37,150
5	33,600	35,300	37,900
6	34,300	36,300	38,600
7	34,800	37,600	39,400
8	35,500	38,300	40,100
9	36,100	39,000	40,850
10	37,500	39,750	41,600
11		40,350	42,300
12		41,100	43,050
13		41,750	43,800
14		42,500	44,500
15		43,100	46,000

Schedule I is a simple index to calculate pay based on teaching certificate and years of experience. As a beginning teacher you hold a provisional certificate. As you gain tenure and advanced training, your certificate and salary improve. Note that experience increments do not increase after year ten unless you have improved your license; then, fifteen years becomes the last experience increment. Also, you must have a number of years of experience before you can have a permanent license.

SAMPLE SALARY SCHEDULE II

Step	BA	BA+30	BA+45 or MA	MA+30	MA+60 Doctorate*
1	31,557	33,202	35,544	37,884	38,999
2	31,771	33,417	35,758	38,098	39,202
3	32,019	33,722	35,910	39,157	39,389
4	32,801	34,505	36,763	39,942	40,175
5	34,278	35,984	37,955	40,420	41,650
6	5,757	36,462	39,435	41,897	43,129
7	37,236	38,942	40,910	43,376	44,609
8	38,713	40,420	42,390	44,853	46,086
9	40,193	41,897	43,867	46,333	47,563
10	42,673	43,376	45,346	47,809	49,042
11	43,148	44,853	46,826	49,288	50,520
12		46,333	48,302	50,767	51,998
13		47,809	49,780	52,244	53,478
14		49,288	51,260	53,724	54,953
15		49,780	51,753	54,216	55,447
16		50,274	52,244	54,708	55,941
17		50,765	52,738	55,200	56,432
18		51,260	53,229	55,694	56,926
19		51,751	53,724	56,186	57,419
20		52,491	54,463	56,926	58,157
21		52,491	54,463	56,926	58,157
22		52,491	54,463	56,926	58,157
23	56,909	58,959	61,520	62,802	63,302

* Doctorate $400 over the MA+ 60 scale. Salary schedule II is more sophisticated. Salary is increased for experience every year, and more incentives are provided for attaining advanced degrees.

Insurance

One of the common fringe benefits with monetary value is health insurance. Few systems pay the total premium; most require a contribution from your pay. The plan may cover doctor visits, prescriptions, and surgical services. Life insurance in an amount equivalent to your yearly salary is often included. Sometimes liability insurance is provided, through either the school system or your professional organization. As a teacher you may be liable for an action, intentional or unintentional; professional liability insurance pays legal fees and represents you in court if you are not sued.

Retirement

As a teacher you are a member of the public employees' or teachers' retirement system in your state. Each pay period you and your school system contribute to the retirement system. Wealthier school systems and states may make the total contribution for you. In most cases, you will make a payroll deduction to the retirement plan. You can retire after twenty-five to thirty years of service in one system. The amount you receive after retirement varies according to your number of years of service and the wealth of the system. Your salary during the last five years of service is often an index for calculating the benefits.

If you leave a state, you are no longer contributing to its retirement system; however, you can withdraw the cash amount you have contributed, as well as take out loans against your balance. Most teachers also contribute to Old Age and Survivors Insurance, commonly called Social Security. This also provides retirement benefits at age sixty-five based upon your contributions. In case of your death, your surviving spouse is eligible for benefits. The amount of social security benefits is small compared to other investment and retirement programs in which you could enroll.

Credit Unions and Investment Programs

A credit union is chartered and insured by the state as a financial organization for its members. Many teachers use the credit union to obtain personal and automobile loans. An automatic deduction can be withheld from your check for the credit union in a savings or investment account. A variety of investment programs such as mutual funds, money markets, and tax deferred savings programs are available through credit unions. The interest rates paid by credit unions are competitive with those of banks.

Summer Vacation

A summer vacation of six to eight weeks is considered a fringe benefit by some teachers. It is often not listed as an official fringe benefit for negotiation. If you manage your funds carefully or take your pay in twelve monthly periods instead of ten, you can relax, travel, study, or write. Many teachers use the summer to take advantage of other employment opportunities either in the education field, such as tutoring, or in an unrelated occupation. Periodically you may choose to use the vacation to work toward an advanced degree or certificate renewal.

Salary Subsidies

As a teacher you may be eligible to receive salary subsidies for work beyond the normal job description. For example, extracurricular activities such as coaching, clubs, in-service attendance, night-class teaching, and development of curriculum and teaching materials can lead to additional salary. Some teachers have found that a combination of summer vacation, holidays, and convenient work hours allows them to maintain part-time jobs or turn hobbies into profit-making ventures.

Leave

A variety of leaves of absence are often available. Sick leave of about ten days a year is often provided as part of your contract; it can be used or accumulated up to a stated number of days. Some days can be contributed to advance your retirement date. Emergency leave of two to three days per year is common. Maternity leave is now a legal requirement for teachers. Family leave policies are being formulated in some places. After a few years of service, you may be eligible for sabbatical leave. This leave can be paid or unpaid and can extend for a semester or a year. It is usually used for further study, travel, or writing.

The purpose of fringe benefits is to attract and retain the best available teachers to the district. Recent improvements in salary and benefits have made teaching an attractive career. If your personal and financial concerns are taken care of, you are better able to concentrate your efforts toward teaching students.

You may be surprised to learn that an experienced first grade teacher can earn more than many college teachers. A college teacher usually moves through these ranks:

1. Lecturer, a part-time instructor who teaches one or more courses per semester; usually a person with particular expertise, such as a president of a local company
2. Instructor, usually a person with less than a doctoral degree who teaches one or more courses per semester
3. Assistant professor, the first rank for a full-time professor with a doctoral degree
4. Associate professor, a promotional step roughly equivalent to achieving tenure in the public schools
5. Full professor, typically the highest rank

Each of these ranks has an approximate salary scale, which follows, like that of public school teachers, although it is often open to more individual negotiation. Most people who choose college teaching do so because they like the flexibility of the schedule, teaching older students, and the required research and publishing activities. The following salary scale for college teaching is from recent estimates of averages.

Lecturer	$31,000
Instructor	36,000
Assistant Professor	45,000
Associate Professor	54,000
Professor	64,000

College teachers receive fringe benefits similar to those of public school teachers. They are usually members of the state employees' or state public school teacher retirement system, insurance system, and credit union. Their contracts may also include a provision that they can serve as consultants with other agencies and schools without taking vacation leave. Some colleges and universities also allow the children of faculty members to attend the institution with no charge for tuition.

Teacher Associations and Unions

Teachers in many of the larger school districts and approximately thirty-five states have the right of collective bargaining. Collective bargaining means that teachers are represented by a professional union in salary and working condition negotiations. These negotiations result in a contract that outlines the conditions of employment for a specified period of time. However, in most states a strike by teachers is still technically illegal because of their status as public employees. Collective bargaining is important because it officially recognizes and protects the rights and responsibilities of the workers.

Two major teacher association/unions operate in the country: the National Education Association (NEA) and the American Federation of Teachers (AFT). The NEA has more than two million members and the AFT has more than 700,000 members. As a professional person you should give serious consideration to joining and participating in your teacher association, as it works for the improvement of the profession as well as your personal interests.

In recent years many national studies have reviewed the status of teaching specifically and education in general. Almost without exception they have recommended that teacher salaries, particularly those at starting levels, must be raised to attract and retain quality teachers. The morale of the teaching force and people's ability to be financially secure are the cornerstone of the educational system. These studies also have recommended plans to improve other aspects of the profession. Two of the recommendations are for merit pay and/or career ladders.

Merit pay, an idea that has been around for years, involves paying teachers for doing an excellent job above and beyond the call of duty. The difficulty with the plan is how to measure excellence in teaching. We can observe teachers according to criteria or we can look at the test scores of their students; however, how can we factor in the impact of the home and differences in students and resources from school to school and year to year? Because there are so many variables, some teachers and teacher associations have been dissatisfied with these plans.

A second recommendation is for a career ladder, which would allow excellent teachers to assume more responsibility within the school system. They could conduct in-service, prepare materials, or mentor beginning teachers, and salaries would be increased accordingly. These plans continue to be tried in states and districts. Thus far, no long-term success has been achieved.

As we move into the twenty-first century, we see the improvement of teacher salaries and working conditions during the past few years as a successful trend that should continue. In many districts, teacher salaries are becoming competitive, when compared to increased contract time and job responsibilities, with supervisory and administrative personnel. This fact is assisting in keeping very talented teachers in the classroom where they are needed and making teaching a financially rewarding career. Perhaps the teacher-reward structures mentioned above or others will succeed in establishing integrity, increasing salaries, and improving working conditions in the teaching profession.

Continuing in Professional Practice

So far we have looked at the preparation, licensure, and beginning year for a new teacher. The time you will have invested by this point is around five years. Now you can look forward to your professional career, which could span a period of twenty to forty years. That time will be invested in the everyday practice of teaching students.

HOW DOES TEACHING DIFFER AT VARIOUS LEVELS?

Have you noticed among your brothers, sisters, and friends that each age group seems to have particular characteristics? Schools, as well as teachers, must take these characteristics into consideration when planning educational programs. The larger divisions of schooling fall into these categories: preschool, which includes ages three, four, and five and the corresponding grade levels of nursery school, prekindergarten, and kindergarten; elementary school, including ages six to nine or six to eleven and grades one through four or six; middle school, ages ten to fourteen and grades five to eight; and junior high school, ages thirteen to fifteen and grades seven to nine. Then come the high school years, grades nine through twelve and ages fifteen to eighteen.

You may have noticed other variations of grades and ages of children, but they have their roots in the developmental characteristics of children.

Within these broad divisions of schooling you will find much variance. Children in grade one are learning to read, while children in grade four are starting to learn various content disciplines. Students in grade five are still considered young and dependent children; students in grade eight are young adults about ready to enter high school. Teachers can describe in detail how each grade level differs from another and how they prefer to teach one or the other of those grades. Any particular group of students also has different interests, attitudes, abilities, and needs, which a good teacher takes into account. Regardless of the grade level or subject you eventually choose to teach, you have a responsibility in common with all teachers. That responsibility is to teach in the most effective and efficient way you can in order to help students develop from dependent to independent persons, both personally and in the mastery of subject matter. Teaching involves personal guidance of students as much as it does the imparting of information.

THE LEVELS OF TEACHING

Preschool

Preschool is a concept that has developed over the years. Originally the term meant children ages three to five who were involved in some type of educational program, usually operated by private or religious schools. During the last ten years these programs, and the need for them, have grown dramatically. The number of working parents and the current baby boom have created a demand for programs that combine quality educational experiences and quality day care.

Kindergarten is now considered part of the regular public school experience, and attendance is required in several states. Prekindergarten for four-year-olds is becoming part of many public school programs. Nursery schools are also increasing in number; these programs for three-year-olds are usually in the private school arena. Kindergarten is a half-day program in many states, but the current trend is toward a full day, with prekindergarten and nursery school programs staying at a half day.

Nursery school programs are experiential, allowing children to manipulate and play with a variety of articles in their environment. The programs are not highly structured, but are highly planned, based upon the children's interests and developmental needs. Goals of a nursery school program might include naming colors, shapes, sizes, and spatial relationships.

Prekindergarten programs for four-year-olds provide developmentally appropriate experiences in the areas of cognitive, emotional, social, and physical growth. Teachers use their observation, experience, and content knowledge to plan a language-rich environment based upon the child's interests. A variety of real-life experiences and materials is provided to meet the wide range of student interests and abilities.

Kindergarten programs have varied over the years according to prevailing educational philosophies. Currently, as a result of pressure from parents and the nature and availability of prekindergarten and nursery school programs, the kindergarten program is becoming more academically oriented. The curriculum emphasizes readiness for first-grade reading and mathematics skills. The activities are much more teacher-directed, as in the rest of the school program, and paper-and-pencil tasks are required for sustained periods of time. Letter names, letter recognition, colors, shapes, sizes, and other relationships are expected of kindergarten students.

Teachers of these groups of children usually are responsible for one group of twenty to twenty-five pupils for the year. In half-day programs a full-time teacher may have two groups. Teachers often have full-time aides who handle administrative work and assist in managing students. Preschool teachers are responsible for all of the subjects to be taught and often must supervise the entire group during lunch. Discipline problems are unlikely at this level, but these young children are not yet adept at controlling their emotions, language, and thought.

ELEMENTARY SCHOOL

The elementary school is still the first contact with formal schooling for more than 10 percent of children. Thus, the elementary teacher faces many challenges. The children must be taught to regulate their behavior to conform to a classroom full of other children. At the same time, the teacher is responsible for teaching the students the fundamentals of reading, writing, and arithmetic. At the end of this division of schooling, students are expected to have mastered the basic skills and be adept at using them to gain information from textbooks in all the subject areas. If students do not reach this achievement level, the rest of their schooling is basically handicapped unless additional assistance is provided.

Several organizational patterns are found in elementary schools. The most common is the self-contained classroom. The elementary teacher is usually responsible for teaching all of the subjects to one group of twenty-five to twenty-eight students. Sometimes extra remedial assistance is available, and many schools provide other teachers for art and music.

Another pattern is the departmentalized plan, under which teachers specialize in one or two subjects and teach only those. The popularity of this plan has moved toward the middle school level in recent years. Another pattern of current vogue is the ungraded plan, used from kindergarten to grade three or four. Students progress at their own rate, with a curriculum or list of objectives to be reached.

Team teaching is an organizational plan that is coming into prominence because of its ability to mesh with teacher merit and career ladder plans. The plan, which has been around in one form or another for years, allows teachers to cooperate and use their individual strengths to meet the needs of students. Students can be assigned to large or small groups or to individual teaching stations.

As a teacher of the lower grades, you need to love working with young children and watching them grow. Teaching at this level is not so much about basic skills as it is about motivating students. A teacher must inspire children and give them the desire to learn. Happily, most children come to school with these traits, and we need only foster them. It is crucial that a teacher at this level know and stay attuned to each student in the class.

Elementary school is typically a very desirable place to work. The building is filled with a love of children, a cooperative atmosphere, and interested students. Thus, you will find most of the innovative programs being tried out in elementary school.

MIDDLE/JUNIOR HIGH SCHOOL

In the early days of education in America, the elementary school ranged from grades one to six, and then through grade eight. Seldom did students go beyond this level of schooling. As schooling became more universal, programs extended more into the high school years. A division of the school continuum called junior high began. In grades seven to nine, the subjects are discrete and are taught by subject specialist teachers, and the program includes intramural athletics, interscholastic athletics, and extracurricular clubs and other activities.

We are now seeing more interest in a middle school concept for grades five to eight. This type of organization combines the best of both the elementary school and the secondary school. Children in the middle school years are becoming more sophisticated and self-reliant, but they are not independent. These students experience the onset of adolescence and all of the problems associated with that growth period. Teachers in the middle schools often can specialize in their content areas. Emphasis is placed on combining related content areas and on cooperation among teachers. Varied activities are provided to students to allow them to make connections within the content and to the world. Clubs are provided that focus on the needs and interests of this age group.

SENIOR HIGH SCHOOL

High school teachers have a different range of responsibilities. They are subject or content specialists who have in-depth knowledge of their areas and seldom teach more than two subjects. Teachers at this level must prepare lessons in more detail because of the sophistication of students.

Senior high students are more self-reliant and independent than are younger students. They require more sophisticated clubs to satisfy a variety of interests. Teachers usually take turns in sponsoring club activities or supervising sports events.

COLLEGE

College-level teaching can be divided roughly into three levels: junior or community colleges, undergraduate colleges or universities, and graduate level universities. The two-year community and junior colleges concentrate mainly on vocational and occupation-oriented programs such as nursing or computer training. The programs emphasize basic skills, with limited humanities or liberal arts courses and heavy concentration on the student's major. These students are principally interested in obtaining employment after graduation; they usually live at home and hold a job to help meet expenses.

College and university teaching usually involves a liberal-arts concept. Students choose the four-year institution to receive both a broad educational background and a vocation or profession for later use. Teachers at this level are generally less concerned with the individual interests or problems of students. Teachers concentrate on either the professional side of a college (medicine, law, education) or the liberal arts side (art, science, mathematics, history). College teaching requires teachers to participate in faculty meetings, committees, social activities, and administration as well as reading, studying, and publishing in their fields.

As you can see, the teacher's day is far from easy. A sincere love of children, a mastery of subject, a willingness to work hard, a knowledge of teaching techniques, and an ability to communicate are the essentials to success in the field of teaching.

Special Hints for the Beginning Teacher
Experienced teachers offer the following tips on getting started as a successful teacher:

- Trust yourself. Your instincts and training have been successful so far. Establish yourself as a confident leader of the class. Try many teaching activities and rely on the ones that feel most comfortable.
- Do not try to be friends with students. Remember, if you are a beginning teacher in a secondary school, you may be only three to five years older than some of your students. You must achieve respect, and students will respect a fair person with standards.
- Plan plenty of work for students. This work should be meaningful and varied. Plentiful and appropriate work improves students' achievement as well as classroom management.
- Be positive. A positive attitude is appreciated by students, teachers, and the administration. Say something nice to students and fellow teachers as often as possible without being phony. Being positive with others also allows you to be positive with yourself. Don't be too hard on yourself in the beginning days of teaching. Success

requires some "on-the-job" training no matter how good your education.

- Communicate with students and colleagues. Talk with your students, which also means to listen to them. Two-way communication may head off potential problems. The same applies to your fellow teachers. Introduce yourself to your colleagues on the first day!

- Be patient. Tomorrow always offers another chance and another perspective on most matters.

- Give clear directions. Failure to give clear directions to students orally and in writing results in a lot of wasted time and energy and poor learning.

- Be prepared for each lesson. Students easily spot a teacher who is "winging it." Planning on a short-range and long-range basis lets students know you are in charge. Being in charge also allows you to capitalize on students' interests and questions.

- Learn to see the entire class. Remember when as a student you thought the teacher must have eyes in the back of his or her head? This is a technique you need to develop. Learn to see the entire class as you are working with a single student or a small group. This is essential to manage the work of the entire class and to maintain a learning atmosphere for all. Lacking this skill, you have to rely on other students' observation to referee any disputes.

- Add variety to the class. Although establishing routines is important, variety within the routine is essential to maintaining student interest (as well as your own).

- Maintain your health. Teaching is a demanding job.

TIPS FOR MANAGEMENT AND DISCIPLINE

The following tips relate to maintaining an orderly and safe environment for learning.

- Establish definite routines. Teachers whose teaching is random and unplanned find themselves in trouble. One of the findings of a recent study of beginning teachers was that much time is lost in switching from one activity to another.
- The following are time-tested administrative procedures:

  Adjust your classroom routines to those of the school at large (punctuality, lunch time, fire drills, hallway procedures, other teachers' schedules).

  Learn the names of your students as soon as possible.

  Use seating arrangements that are appropriate for the type of class and students.

  Start and stop your lessons by your schedule. Don't let the bell close your class.

  Move around the class during each session. Don't sit behind your desk.

- Make only promises and threats that you are prepared to carry out. Gradually you learn the nature of each of the students, and they in turn learn yours. If you promise a test, give the test. If you threaten a punishment, be prepared to carry out the punishment. (Also know whether the administration will back your threat.) If students learn that you are bluffing, you lose their respect and, more important, control of the class.

- Establish clear policies and rules. Do not make too many rules because you cannot remember them, much less enforce them.
- Use common sense. Again, as in most areas, trust your training, judgment, and common sense when both positive and negative situations occur.
- Be fair and consistent. Inconsistency with students leads to problems in management and teaching.
- Don't argue with students. Know the difference between productive communication and argument.
- Don't talk about one student with another student. Share information only with persons who have a need to know.
- Manage instructional and administrative time. "Downtime" allows for the possibility of problems occurring. Keep the pace of activity continuous and brisk.
- Maintain a safe and orderly physical environment. Attention to the details of your classroom environment not only gives the impression of organization but contributes to true organization. Decorate your room!
- Build a community atmosphere among students. This will establish a climate of respect for individuals and reduce antagonisms.
- Learn and practice how to take part in positive interventions and conflict resolution strategies with students.

Tips for Instruction

Interacting with students is the reason you become a teacher and the major reward in your career. However, teaching requires skills and strategies to be honed over a lifetime. The following tips along with your teacher training, will help you get started. Let's start from the general and move to the more specific.

Your instructional yearly, monthly, weekly, and daily planning is important. School districts and states usually provide curriculum guides or instructional frameworks that outline skills, knowledge, and abilities each student is to obtain. These guides are often organized by subject and grade level. This is the beginning point for your planning. Instruction must be paced according to student needs and abilities in light of the amount of content to be covered. Student learning should be your guide. It does no good to cover a lot of content unless the students are demonstrating their learning. You must scope out the entire year and then begin organizing monthly plans. Many useful planning formats and materials are available for assistance.

Weekly and daily planning require you to be more specific. Many schools will need you to give your weekly and daily lesson plans in writing. This requirement forces you to plan ahead, and it leaves a record for the times you may be ill and a substitute teacher must be hired to replace you.

All of your activities during the day have an impact on the quality of instruction. Your day must be organized to minimize time lost to handing out papers or the transitions among instructional activities. It is important each day to build in routine activities that provide a foundation of expectations for students as well as streamline your practices. Begin each day with students with a friendly greeting to establish an atmosphere of trust. Opening activities can relate to the instructional goals of the day or to current events that may be on the students' minds. Also, closing activities for the day can be useful. Remember, however, that your job is to teach students.

The following lesson plan framework is an example that can help you organize every instructional lesson. Most lesson plans contain the following components:

- Topic of the lesson
- Opening activity
- Lesson objectives for students to achieve
- Instructional strategies to achieve objectives
- Guided practice by students
- Independent practice by students
- Closure activities
- Student evaluation to check for student understanding.

Tips for Collegial Relationships

It is important to develop a collegial relationship with other teachers. You will find them a valuable resource when problems arise. Don't let problems grow before you seek assistance. Decisive action is important in managing students on a daily basis.

Learn to ask questions when you don't know. Don't guess; be certain. This applies to rules, practices, traditions—written or unwritten.

You also can help yourself by involving parents in your classroom. This is a continual process that will build goodwill with parents when you need their support in negative situations.

Finally, if you are not assigned a mentor, find one of your own. Study successful teachers in order to learn.

Why Some Teachers Are Not Successful

Surveys of students show that they rate teachers low if they:

- Ridicule a student in front of the class
- Shout at the class
- Lose their tempers
- Lack a sense of humor
- Consistently talk down to or over the heads of the students
- Lecture all the time and do not vary class procedures; act like a "know-it-all"

Most teachers who fail do so because they fail to establish successful routines with the school and the students. A lack of content knowledge is seldom the reason for failure. Teaching is a human resource activity that involves managing students on a daily basis, and each day will have its share of successful and unsuccessful situations.

WHAT NONTEACHING ASSIGNMENTS WILL YOU RECEIVE?

The types and difficulties of nonteaching duties depend on the size of the school, the grade levels taught, the type of administrative organization, the ability level of the students, the volunteer program, and the number and level of courses offered.

Nonteaching assignments generally fall into the following categories:

"Housekeeping" duties:
hall duty, cafeteria duty, playground duty, and bus duty.

Advisory duty:
high school class, student government, and student adviser.

Sponsoring:
school organizations, parent organizations.

Mentoring:
As part of the orientation program for new teachers, many schools assign an experienced teacher as a "buddy" to assist each new teacher with questions, routines, materials, curriculum, and any other personal or professional issues during orientation.

Doing nonpaid administrative assignments:
Some principals assist aspiring administrators by allowing them to share in certain administrative duties, such as helping with the school's master schedule, developing an administrative handbook, rewriting the curriculum, and making special presentations at faculty meetings.

Working with student teachers:
Many schools that are near a teacher training college or university have the opportunity to assist with the teaching program. Teachers who are selected to receive student teachers from the university normally work with these students for six to twelve weeks. The assignment involves teaching demonstration lessons, helping students prepare and carry out lesson plans, supervising the student's teaching and giving post-lesson critiques, and maintaining communication with the college.

Monitoring:
study hall, homeroom period, athletic contests, school dances, dinners, and other social events, and graduation.

Contacting the home:
Most elementary and secondary schools have procedures for telephoning the home when a student is

involved in a serious problem, is absent for two or more days, or is in danger of failing a subject, and conversely when a student has shown marked improvement or has done something outstanding. This type of assignment is often shared by teachers and parent volunteers and increasingly by automated telephone systems and computer networks.

Conducting research and publishing:
If you teach at a college or university, you will probably be expected to do research work related to your field of expertise. Your future promotions may depend upon the number and quality of your publications.

Nonteaching assignments may not be a teacher's favorite part of the job, but they are essential to the smooth operation of all schools, public or private, elementary through university. Your participation in these assignments gives you invaluable experience, gives you added rapport with students and colleagues, and pays dividends by improving the quality of your school. In the long run, it will even make your job easier!

HOW WILL HIGH-TECH HELP YOU?
One of the most pervasive elements in our society is also affecting the schools. That element is technology. Technology here refers to the high technologies that have improved medicine, science, space travel, and the business world.

Current examples of technology in the schools include:

- Educational/cable television
- Computer labs
- Telecommunications through computer modems

- Multimedia presentations on videodiscs
- Videotape recorders
- Telecommunications through satellites
- Internet

Older technologies such as audiotape recorders, radios, televisions, cameras, records, filmstrip projectors, and 16 mm films have been staples in the schools for years.

Technology and the Student

Technology opens up a whole new world of possibilities for the individual student. Learning does not need to be confined to the school day. Television, home computers, calculators, and cable television all have contributed to changing the way we learn. For instance, calculators have eliminated the need to do longhand calculations or complex equations. Should we make students take the long way to solve complex problems in the classroom or allow them to use the technology?

The answer is that students probably should be taught to do longhand calculations to learn the mathematical processes involved, then be allowed to use the technology. The same is true of word processors. Word processing programs now correct grammar and spelling errors. Students can spend more time thinking about the content of their writing than about the mechanics. But should we stop teaching grammar and handwriting in the schools? Probably not, especially since software programs are not foolproof.

Instead of memorizing information, students can let technology do the memory storage and spend more time in problem-solving, reasoning, and gaining a better understanding of complicated problems. Technology allows students to work cooperatively to explore the solutions to real-life situations, which usually have more than one answer. The Bureau of Labor Statistics predicts the majority of future jobs will require computer literacy skills. It is incumbent on prospective teachers to become computer literate and incorporate technologies of all types into the school program.

WHAT SPECIALIZED POSITIONS ARE AVAILABLE?

If you are looking forward to working in the field of education, but are still undecided on whether you want to be a teacher for thirty years or more, there are many specialized positions to consider. Each school system uses many professional staff members to supplement the work of the classroom teacher.

Specialists cover a broad range of duties and responsibilities, similar to those of a large corporation. Included are:

Management
Specialists in management fill positions from the top manager, the superintendent or president, to the middle managers, to principals or deans, to project directors, and administrative assistants.

Finance
Personnel in this category work with budget planning, supervision of expenditures, and purchasing of supplies and materials.

Personnel

Specialists in the personnel department are essential to recruit the best possible candidates for teaching positions. These specialists also assist the local school with maintaining high morale in the school district.

Supervision

Many school systems employ supervisors in special subject areas, to help the principal and teachers maintain quality instruction.

Curriculum

To keep the school system responsive to the changing needs of society and new information in subject matter fields, curriculum specialists are needed.

Health and Social Services

Both health and social services require specialists to work with students and parents.

Disabled

Specialists are needed to work with disabled students, including those with special learning, speech, emotional, physical, sight, and hearing needs.

Special Subject Matter

Specialists are assigned to teach those unique subjects that are not taught by the classroom teacher. Music and art are two examples.

Human Resources

This group includes pupil personnel workers, counselors, staff development and training, and employee assistance program personnel. Dealing with the variety of teacher and student problems requires the assistance of specially trained personnel.

Adult Education and Parent Education

Most school systems have adopted the philosophy that education is an ongoing process from infancy to death, and they make provisions for adult education classes. In addition, some federal programs require that parents be actively involved in the education of students.

Testing and Research

The public as well as teachers and students are interested in seeing progress. Recent reform efforts have focused on assessment and accountability of student performance. This has led to an increase in testing and research units in school systems.

Library/Media

The school library or media center is described by some educators as the "heart of the learning program." Both students and teachers depend on the extensiveness of the print and nonprint collection and services of the library media center.

Public Relations

In addition to the information sent out by the local school, most school systems depend on a trained person or persons to "tell the story" of what is going on in the schools and to communicate with the local paper and television stations.

Technology

With the ever-increasing use of computers in administration, finance, and instruction, the need for trained experts to keep the "systems" operating is essential.

Some larger school districts have been assigned one or more cable television channels. Trained personnel are needed for the programming and operation of this useful communication tool.

All of these specialists need to be able to relate their services to the important work of the classroom teacher. For obvious reasons, eligibility for many of these positions requires previous classroom teaching experience.

Business and Industry

The leaders of business and industry have recognized the necessity of working with schools to ensure that graduates are better prepared for the world of work. Liaison personnel help to coordinate these programs in the schools.

Specialists in the Local School

The number and variety of specialists assigned to the local school depend on the grade levels served, the number of students, the demands and expectations of the community, and the level of financial support in a school district. Schools in wealthy districts have a smaller student-teacher ratio, offer more choices in the curriculum, and employ more subject matter specialists. Some of the specialists may be assigned on a part-time basis so that they can serve two or more schools.

The typical school staff includes specialists in the categories of special subjects, special services, special education, federal programs, operational support, and administration. The positions that are normally found in these categories include:

Special subjects: art, vocal music, instrumental music, foreign languages, physical education, librarian/media, computer/technology, and learning specialist.

The classification of "special" is restricted to the elementary school, since the areas mentioned are usually taught by a staff member other than the classroom teacher. In secondary schools and colleges they are considered a regular part of the curriculum, since the administrative pattern of the school is departmentalization.

In secondary schools, the remedial reading teacher might be in charge of a reading clinic and might also teach a course in speed reading. Some secondary schools offer an entire curriculum of special subjects, including performing arts, vocational-technical, science and technology, and alternative education (programs for students with severe adjustment problems).

Special services: guidance counselor, psychologist, pupil personnel worker, home and hospital teacher, social worker, school nurse, and dietitian.

The specialists who are in this category work with both students and parents. The position of dietitian might be combined with that of cafeteria manager. Pupil personnel workers provide liaisons between the school and the home for students with attendance or behavior problems or in need of social services. Home and hospital teachers work with students who are confined to a hospital or the home.

Special education: teacher of learning-disabled students, speech and hearing specialist, sight saving specialist, physical therapist, and occupational therapist.

Some of these specialists work in self-contained classrooms; others work with smaller groups or individual students. Teachers of learning-disabled students work with levels of disability ranging from slight to extreme.

Special education teachers also work with physically and emotionally challenged students along with other specialists including the school psychologist and pupil services worker. In some schools special education students are "mainstreamed," or grouped with regular students during one or more periods of the school day.

Federal Programs

For the past two decades, federal funds have been available to schools to assist with programs for students who are educationally or physically disadvantaged or both. One of the best known is Head Start, a preschool program designed to prepare children from disadvantaged backgrounds for elementary school.

Other federal programs give added assistance to students in various areas, such as reading and mathematics, bilingual classes, college preparatory classes, dropout prevention, and finding summer employment. Many programs also are designed to help the school system implement desegregation mandates.

The types of specialists in federal programs cover a wide range, because of the variety of programs that have been funded to meet local needs. This specialist needs to understand program design, implementation, and evaluation.

Enrichment Programs: talented and gifted (TAG), environmental education, college preparatory, and language development.

Operational Support: transportation specialists, food service specialists, and business/finance specialists.

Administration: principal, headmaster, vice-principal, dean, administrative assistant, department chairperson, and grade chairperson.

Specialists at the Area and Central Office Level

Specialists who work in an area office or in the central office of the school system have supervisory responsibility for many staff members. School systems that cover a large geographical area use area offices as administrative units. These specialists have received appointment through demonstrated competence in their fields, and most have had years of successful teaching experience.

Many teachers consider the specialized positions as promotions or advancements up the career ladder, since they usually involve a twelve-month contract and higher salary, allow for a twenty-five-day vacation each year, offer more freedom than classroom teaching, and carry a perceived higher prestige factor.

Bear in mind that successful classroom teaching, usually for a minimum of three to five years, is a prerequisite for appointment to any specialized position. The point of view and perspective of the classroom teacher are still invaluable qualifications, to keep the field of education on a sound foundation.

Emerging Challenges in Teaching

In addition to the improvement of salary, working conditions, professional autonomy, and other social influences, the profession is facing one of the most dramatic changes in the student population in the country's history since the early waves of immigration. These challenges will change the definition and role of the teacher of the future. If you are considering becoming a teacher, you need to consider the impact of the following information.

CHANGING STUDENT NEEDS

A major challenge affecting teaching is the changing needs of the students entering the schools. The increased number of students entering the schools is one factor. Not since the baby boomers born in the late 1940s have the schools seen such a population growth. Those baby boomers have been establishing families and having children while they were in their late thirties. This has resulted in a small baby boom and a "bubble," or swell, in the population of children to be educated. That "bubble" is now in the middle and secondary school levels. The impact on education has been the need for additional school construction, teachers, and resources, which in turn must be shifted within the systems in order to provide a quality education as the bubble moves through the system.

Another challenge to the school systems is to provide integrated health, social, and instructional services to a population of students who have special needs beyond the average student. School systems must provide adequate early childhood programs in order to invite students to educational experiences both inside and outside their homes before they reach six to eight years of age.

Another challenge that future teachers will face is that by the year 2010, a large city school district may have children who have more than one hundred language backgrounds. Methods such as bilingual education and English as a Second Language (ESL) are used effectively in these systems, but these students will remain a significant challenge to teachers and school systems in the future.

Current estimates in this country are that at least one in four students entering the public schools is living at or below the poverty level of income. Also related to this trend is the fact that the family structure is changing in this country. There is a great chance that many of these students will live at least a portion of their lives with only one parent.

Another group of students whose number is on the increase in the public schools is those with physical and/or mental disabilities. In the past, these students often were separated from the regular school population and taught in special rooms by special teachers. Now, many students who are less disabled are placed in the regular classroom. As a result, many states require courses in special education for all prospective and current teachers.

Dropout rates are also a problem. The nation's schools currently graduate about 88 percent of the number of students who enter the ninth grade. Some rural and suburban school districts have smaller dropout rates, but some urban schools have 40 to 50 percent dropout rates.

Problems of society such as random violence, teenage pregnancy, substance abuse, poor health and nutrition, and social diseases also show up at the school door. Schools are often expected to solve all of these problems through good programs and instruction; however, school improvement is only part of the solution. Schooling must be a community and societal effort to be successful.

We do have signs that student achievement is improving in some areas and that schools are succeeding with some students. Evidence indicates that students in the last decade are taking more challenging courses in the secondary schools. Current efforts to establish higher standards for students and improved instructional methods should continue the trend toward improved student learning.

Your Exciting Future in Teaching

The central theme of this book has been to provide both a realistic and an optimistic picture of teaching as a possible career. Teaching has changed dramatically during the past century, from the days of the one-room school (where the teacher also performed custodial duties) to today's modern classrooms, with the availability of numerous forms of technology to assist in the teaching-learning process. There has never been a better time to enter the field of teaching, with the rewards and opportunities that lie ahead for those who are successful.

You should make your career decision based on your own insights, the background you have gained in school, discussions with your parents and counselor, and the information you have gained through reading this book. Whatever you decide, remember that teaching is a challenge that promises to be most rewarding to you in the future.

GOOD NEWS

There are many reasons to be optimistic about the state of education and teaching in this country. Although teachers are often criticized by the educational reform movement, that same criticism is resulting in improvements and good news.

According to assessment results of the National Assessment of Educational Progress, the basic skills abilities of students, particularly young minority students, have improved as a result of the increased emphasis. Much remains to be accomplished, but we can take heart that the educational system can respond and make improvements when given adequate time and resources.

Another bright side to the educational picture is that the importance of teachers in school reform and society is being recognized and rewarded. More money has been appropriated for salaries and programs. Attention to class size, teacher involvement in school operations, concentration on curriculum, teaching, learning, assessment, and standards and goals for the nation all hold promise for the teaching profession.

We are in a period of educational reform that may be the most beneficial to teachers ever. The current wave of reform includes standards as one of its banners (standards for the content to be taught and standards for the level of achievement desired of students). Emphasis is on raising the standards on which the content and achievement of educational progress are measured. Concentration has moved from the basic skills to the higher-order thinking skills necessary to function in the twenty-first century. Assessment is then based on these standards as applied to real-world situations and work-related activities.

We have reason to be optimistic that the next decade may offer real and substantive improvement for the teaching profession in terms of the tangible rewards of salary and benefits, the ability to help students through increased resources, and the improvement of the professional status and recognition of teachers.

AN EXCITING FUTURE?

If you have made the decision to try becoming a teacher, you will be joining about 3.5 million others who work in the education profession. You will be a member of one of the largest professions in the United States. Your fellow professionals will include administrators, consultants, supervisors, researchers, college professors, specialists, support personnel, staff members of professional organizations, and, most important, other classroom teachers. Their assignments range from preschool through graduate school, and they will work in public and private institutions and with the state and federal governments.

We are still in an era in which a lot of people think that education is "broken" and needs fixing. It is amazing how many "experts" have "solutions" for improving the schools, such as school vouchers, schools administered by private corporations, more money; reduced class size; copying the Japanese, German, or English system of education; mandatory examinations as graduation requirements; national teacher exams to screen out poor teachers; substance abuse curriculum; sex education curriculum; values education; computer literacy; raising the entry and exit age of compulsory school attendance; and more mathematics and science courses. The list of solutions seems to grow with each passing year.

These days there are serious problems facing schools, teachers and students, but researchers have documented the fact that our schools still get high marks from the public on the job which is being accomplished. Whenever tragedies occur in a school community, the public re-examines how the schools are being administered. Education still needs to update itself continually to address the needs of students and teachers who will live and work well into the twenty-first century. Teachers must raise the standards of the profession in order to achieve the status, recognition, and working conditions they deserve. There are student problems that face tomorrow's new teachers. Among these problems are the effects of broken homes, child abuse, poverty, inadequate funding, crime, dropouts, violence in the schools, substance abuse, teenage pregnancy, suicide, and lack of parental involvement in education.

As a new teacher in the classroom, you will find that in spite of the problems, students still have many of the same interests, emotions, and drives that they have always had. They want to succeed, they need to fit in with their peers, and they want to be loved and respected. They still relate well to teachers who like students, who like to teach, who know their subjects, who know how to teach, and who are both firm and fair. Research in both education and technology has continued to bring new techniques and new equipment into the classroom to help teachers teach and students learn. Advances are being made in the cognitive sciences about how students learn. This will improve the ability of the teacher and the materials of instruction.

We can look into a crystal ball and try to predict the future and the status of the teaching profession. In reality, though, we must create a vision of what needs to be accomplished so that we can start to work. The real challenge is to help achieve this vision and improve the teaching profession and opportunities for students.

Nobel Peace Prize winner Albert Schweitzer wrote in his autobiography, "Every great man was influenced in his life by a great teacher." Yes, teaching does promise an exciting career, and you can be the teacher to influence a great man or woman, if you have what it takes.

Accept the challenge—teach!

Glossary

advisory duty Acting as an adviser for a high school class, student government, or individual students.

alternative school A school that offers programs for disruptive or dropout-prone students.

bachelor of arts (BA) or bachelor of science (BS) Four-year undergraduate degrees, either of which, when completed with a concentration in education, is considered the minimum for licensure and certification in the teaching field.

certification A voluntary advanced process of teacher recognition by a self-governing board (often used synonymously with licensure).

chairperson A teacher who is selected to act as a leader for his or her grade level, department, or committee.

classes for the exceptional student Classes for the talented and gifted (TAG classes) or students with learning difficulties; either grouped together as their own elementary schools, or offered in addition to regular classes.

comprehensive high school The most common secondary school model, in which all services and programs are offered on the same campus.

credit union A financial organization that provides a variety of investment programs for its members, who contribute to the union through automatic deductions from their paychecks.

doctor of philosophy (PhD) or doctor of education (EdD) Advanced degrees obtained by those wanting to teach college, do research, or work toward higher-level administrative positions.

focus school A specialized elementary school offering concentrations on particular subjects while also teaching traditional subjects.

housekeeping duties Teachers' responsibilities for supervising students on school grounds, such as on the playground or in the cafeteria.

magnet school A specialized secondary school for students in subjects such as the performing arts or science and technology.

master of arts (M.A.) or master of science (M.S.) Advanced degrees awarded after approximately one year of full-time graduate study.

mentoring An experienced teacher assisting a new teacher, for example, by answering questions about personal or professional issues.

monitoring Supervising a homeroom or extracurricular events.

nonpaid administrative assignments Administrative jobs that teachers take on if they are considering becoming administrators.

NTE (National Teachers Examination) A written test for prospective teachers, covering both subject matters and pedagogy.

open school An elementary or secondary school in which students are allowed to learn at their own pace and according to their own interests.

restructuring movement A movement to reorganize a school's operation in every way in order to be successful in the future.

salary subsidies Additional salary for work performed beyond the normal job description, such as sponsoring an extracurricular activity.

science and technology center A secondary school that offers courses in higher-level mathematics, pre-engineering technology, advanced science, and technology.

sponsoring Giving assistance to school clubs or parent organizations.

student teacher A teacher in training who works in a classroom for six to twelve weeks.

teaching license (licensure) The permit that either the state department of education or state standards board grants to a teacher in order for him or her to practice in that state.

team teaching Two or more teachers working together to teach a large number of students.

tenure Status granted to a teacher after a probationary period of one to three years, ensuring that the teacher cannot be dismissed or demoted unless he or she violates certain legal rules.

traditional self-contained school An elementary school in which the teacher and students are assigned to a room for a particular grade or level of instruction.

vocational-technical center A secondary school that offers training in a specific trade.

Appendix I
Directory of State Teacher Certification Agencies

IN THE UNITED STATES

Alabama
Teacher Education and Certification Office
State Department of Education
P. O. Box 302101
Montgomery, AL 2101
(334) 242-9977

Alaska
Teacher Certification
State Department of Education
Gold Belt Building
801 West 10th Street
Juneau, AK 99801-1894
(907) 465-8661

Arizona
Teacher Certification Unit
State Department of Education
P. O. Box 6490
Phoenix, AZ 85007
(602) 542-4367

Arkansas
Teacher Education and Licensure
State Department of Education
State Capitol Mall

Little Rock, AR 72201
(501) 682-4342

California
Commission on Teacher Credentialing
1812 Ninth Street
Sacramento, CA 95814-7000
(916) 445-7254

Colorado
Teacher Education and Certification Unit
State Department of Education
201 East Colfax Avenue
Denver, CO 80203
(303) 866-6628

Connecticut
Bureau of Certification and Professional Development
State Department of Education
P.O. Box 2219
Hartford, CT 06145
(203) 566-8289

Delaware
Professional Development and Certification Division
State Department of Public Instruction
Townsend Building
Dover, DE 19903
(302) 739-4686

District of Columbia
Teacher Education and Certification
215 G Street NE
Washington, DC 20002
(202) 724-4246

Florida
Bureau of Teacher Certification
State Department of Education
325 West Gaines Street
Tallahassee, FL 32399
(904) 488-2317

Georgia
Professional Standards Commission
1452 Twin Towers East
Atlanta, GA 30334
(404) 657-9000

Hawaii
Certification and Recruitment Branch
State Department of Education
P.O. Box 2360
Honolulu, HI 96804
(808) 586-3276

Idaho
Teacher Education and Certification
State Department of Education
650 West State Street
Boise, ID 83720
(208) 332-6881

Illinois
Division of Professional Preparation
State Board of Education
100 North First Street
Springfield, IL 62777
(217) 782-2805

Indiana
Professional Standards Board
251 East Ohio Street
Indianapolis, IN 46204
(317) 232-9010

Iowa
Board of Educational Examiners
State Department of Education
Grimes State Office Building
Des Moines, IA 50319-0146
(515) 281-3245

Kansas
Certification, Teacher Education, and Accreditation
State Department of Education
120 S.E. 10th Street
Topeka, KS 66612
(913) 296-2288

Kentucky
Teacher Education and Certification
State Department of Education
1024 Capitol Center Drive
Frankfort, KY 40601
(502) 573-4606

Louisiana
Bureau of Higher Education and Teacher Certification
State Department of Education
P.O. Box 94064
Baton Rouge, LA 70804-9064
(504) 342-3490

Maine
Division of Certification and Placement
State Department of Education
State House Station 23
Augusta, ME 04333
(207) 287-5944

Maryland
Division of Certification and Accreditation
State Department of Education
200 West Baltimore Street
Baltimore, MD 21201
(410) 767-0100

Massachusetts
Office of Teacher Certification and Credentialing
350 Main Street
Malden, MA 02148
(617) 388-3380

Michigan
Teacher Certification
State Department of Education
P.O. Box 30008
Lansing, MI 48909
(517) 373-3310

Minnesota
Professional Licensing
550 Cedar Street
St. Paul, MN 55101
(612) 296-2046

Mississippi
Division of Teacher Certification

State Department of Education
P.O. Box 771
Jackson, MS 39205
(601) 359-3483

Missouri
Teacher Certification
Department of Elementary and Secondary Education
P.O. Box 480
Jefferson City, MO 65102
(314) 751-3486

Montana
Certification Department
Office of Public Instruction
State Capitol
Helena, MT 59620
(406) 444-3150

Nebraska
Teacher Certification
State Department of Education
301 Centennial Mall South
Lincoln, NE 68509-4987
(402) 471-2496

Nevada
Teacher Education and Licensure
State Department of Education
1820 East Sahara
Las Vegas, NV 89104
(702) 486-6455

New Hampshire
Bureau of Credentialing

State Department of Education
101 Pleasant Street
Concord, NH 03301
(603) 271-2407

New Jersey
Division of Professional Development and Licensing
State Department of Education CN 503
Trenton, NJ 08625-0503
(609) 984-1216

New Mexico
Professional Licensure Unit
State Department of Education
Education Building
Santa Fe, NM 87501-2786
(505) 827-6587

New York
Office of Teaching-Certification
State Department of Education
Cultural Education Center
Nelson A. Rockefeller Empire State Plaza
Albany, NY 12230
(518) 474-3901

North Carolina
Licensure Section
State Department of Public Instruction
301 North Wilmington Street
Raleigh, NC 27601-2825
(919) 733-4125

North Dakota
Division of Teacher Certification

State Department of Public Instruction
600 East Boulevard Avenue
Bismarck, ND 58505-0440
(701) 328-2264

Ohio
Division of Teacher Education and Certification
State Department of Education
65 South Front Street
Columbus, OH 43215-4183
(614) 466-3593

Oklahoma
Professional Standards Section
State Department of Education
2500 North Lincoln Boulevard
Oklahoma City, OK 73105-4599
(405) 521-3337

Oregon
Teacher Standards and Practices Commission
255 Capitol Street, NE
Salem, OR 97310
(503) 378-3586

Pennsylvania
Bureau of Teacher Preparation and Certification
State Department of Education
333 Market Street
Harrisburg, PA 17126-0333
(717) 787-2967

Rhode Island
Office of Teacher Education and Certification
Shepard Building

255 Westminster Street
Providence, RI 02903
(401) 277-2675

South Carolina
Teacher Licensure Section
1015 Rutledge Building
Columbia, SC 29201
(803) 734-4600

South Dakota
Division of Education/Teacher Certification
1600 Gervain Street
Pierre, SD 57501-2293
(605) 773-3553

Tennessee
Office of Teacher Licensing
1710 James Robertson Parkway
Nashville, TN 37243-0377
(615) 532-4885

Texas
State Board for Education Certification
1001 Trinity
Austin, TX 78701
(512) 469-7740

Utah
Teacher Certification
State Office of Education
250 East 500 South
Salt Lake City, UT 84111
(801) 538-7740

Vermont
Licensing Office
State Department of Education
120 State Street
Montpelier, VT 05620
(802) 828-2445

Virginia
Teacher Education and Certification
State Department of Education
P.O. Box 2120
Richmond, VA 23216-2120
(804) 225-2022

Washington
Professional Education and Certification
Superintendent of Public Instruction
P.O. Box 47200
Olympia, WA 98504
(360) 753-6773

West Virginia
Office of Professional Preparation
State Department of Education
Capitol Complex
Building 6, Room B-337
Charleston, WV 25305
(304) 348-7010

Wisconsin
Licensing Team
State Department of Public Instruction
P.O. Box 7841
Madison, WI 53707
(608) 266-1027

Wyoming
Professional Standards Board
State Department of Education
Hathaway Building
Cheyenne, WY 82002
(307) 777-6261

Appendix II
Education–Related Organizations

American Association of Colleges for Teacher Education
One Dupont Circle NW
Washington, DC 20036-2412
(202) 293-2450

American Association of Community Colleges
One Dupont Circle NW
Washington, DC 20036-2412
(202) 728-0200

American Association of Educators in Private Practice
N7425 Switzke Road
Watertown, WI 53094
(800) 252-3280

American Association of School Administrators
1801 North Moore Street
Arlington, VA 22209
(703) 528-0700

American Association of School Librarians
50 East Huron Street
Chicago, IL 60611
(312) 944-6780
(800) 545-2433

American Association of State Colleges and Universities
One Dupont Circle NW
Washington, DC 20036-2412
(202) 293-7070

American Association of University Professors
1012 14th Street NW
Washington, DC 20005
(202) 737-5900

American Council on Education
One Dupont Circle NW
Washington, DC 20036-2412
(202) 939-9300

American Federation of Teachers
555 New Jersey Avenue NW
Washington, DC 20001
(202) 879-4400

American Field Service AFS International/Intercultural Programs
220 East 43rd Street
New York, NY 10017
(800) AFS-INFO (237-4636)
(212) 949-4242

Appalachia Educational Laboratory
P.O. Box 1348
Charleston, WV 25325-1348
(800) 624-9120

Carnegie Foundation for the Advancement of Teaching
1755 Massachusetts Avenue NW
Washington, DC 20036
(202) 387-7200

Center for Research on Evaluation, Standards, and Student Testing
UCLA Graduate School of Education
301 GSE&IS Bldg., Box 152206
Los Angeles, CA 90095-1522
(310) 206-1532

Center for Social Organization of Schools
The Johns Hopkins University
3003 North Charles Street
Baltimore, MD 21218
(410) 516-8800

Educational Testing Service
Rosedale Road
Princeton, NJ 08541
(609) 921-9000

Eisenhower National Clearinghouse for Mathematics and Science Education
The Ohio State University
1929 Kenny Road
Columbus, OH 43210-1079
(614) 292-7784

ERIC Clearinghouse on Community Colleges
University of California at Los Angeles
405 Hilgard Avenue
Los Angeles, CA 90024-1564
(213) 825-3931

ERIC Clearinghouse on Counseling and Student Services
University of North Carolina at Greensboro
101 Park Building
Greensboro, NC 27412
(910) 334-4114

ERIC Clearinghouse on Disabilities and Gifted Children
Council for Exceptional Children
1920 Association Drive
Reston, VA 22091-1589
(703) 264-9474

ERIC Clearinghouse on Languages and Linguistics
Center for Applied Linguistics
1118 22nd Street NW
Washington, DC 20037-0037
(202) 429-9551

ERIC Clearinghouse on Reading and Communication Skills
Indiana University
2805 East 10th Street
Bloomington, IN 47408-2373
(812) 855-5847

ERIC Clearinghouse on Rural and Small Schools
Appalachia Educational Laboratory
1031 Quarrier Street
Charleston, WV 25325-1348
(304) 347-0400
(800) 624-9120

ERIC Clearinghouse on Social Studies/Social Science Education
Social Studies Development Center
2805 East 10th Street
Bloomington, IN 47408-2373
(812) 855-3838

ERIC Clearinghouse on Teaching and Teacher Education
American Association of Colleges for Teacher Education
One Dupont Circle NW
Washington, DC 20036-2412
(202) 293-2450

Fulbright Teacher Exchange Program
U.S. Information Agency
301 Fourth Street SW
Washington, DC 20547
(202) 619-4555

Future Educators of America
c/o Phi Delta Kappa
408 North Union
Bloomington, IN 47407
(812) 339-1156

Mid-Continent Regional Educational Laboratory
2550 South Parker Road
Aurora, CO 80014
(303) 337-0990

National Assessment of Educational Progress
P.O. Box 6710
Princeton, NJ 08541
(609) 734-1624

**National Association of State Boards of
Education**
1012 Cameron Street
Alexandria, VA 22314
(703) 684-4000

**National Association of State Directors of
Teacher Education and Certification**
3600 Whitman Avenue North
Seattle, WA 98103
(206) 547-0437

**National Board for Professional Teaching
Standards**
300 River Place
Detroit, MI 48207
(313) 259-0830

**National Center for Restructuring Education,
Schools, and Teaching**
Columbia University
525 West 120th Street
New York, NY 10027
(212) 678-3432

National Council of Teachers of English
1111 Kenyon Road
Urbana, IL 61801
(217) 328-3870

National Education Association
1201 16th Street NW
Washington, DC 20036
(202) 833-4000

National PTA
200 L Street NW
Washington, DC 20036
(202) 331-1380

National School Boards Association
1680 Duke Street
Alexandria, VA 22314
(703) 838-6722

National Science Teachers Association
1840 Wilson Boulevard
Arlington, VA 22201
(703) 243-7100

New England Comprehensive Assistance Center
Education Development Center, Inc.
55 Chapel Street
Newton, MA 02158-1060
(617) 618-2533

North Central Regional Educational Laboratory
1900 Spring Road
Oak Brook, IL 60521
(708) 571-4700

Northwest Regional Educational Laboratory
101 SW Main Street
Portland, OR 97204
(503) 275-9500

Recruiting New Teachers
385 Concord Avenue
Belmont, MA 02178
(617) 489-6000

Research for Better Schools
444 North Third Street
Philadelphia, PA 19123-4107
(215) 574-9300

SouthEastern Regional Vision for Education
P.O. Box 5367
Greensboro, NC 27435
(800) 755-3277

Southwest Educational Development Laboratory
211 East Seventh Street
Austin, TX 78701
(512) 476-6861

Teachers of English to Speakers of Other Languages
1600 Cameron Street
Alexandria, VA 22314
(703) 836-0704

Teach for America
20 Exchange Place
New York, NY 10005
(212) 425-9039

U.S. Department of Education
National Center for Education Statistics
555 New Jersey Avenue NW
Washington, DC 20208
(202) 219-1651
(800) 424-1616

WestEd
730 Harrison Street
San Francisco, CA 94107-1242
(415) 565-3000

IN CANADA

TEACHERS' ASSOCIATIONS

British Columbia Teachers' Federation
100-550 West 6th Avenue
Vancouver, BC V5Z 4P2
(604) 871-2283
Web site: http://www.bctf.bc.ca

Newfoundland and Labrador Teachers' Association
3 Kenmount Road
St. John's, Newfoundland A1B 1W1
(709) 726-3223
Web site: http://www.nlta.nf.ca

Nova Scotia Teachers' Union
3106 Dutch Village Road
Halifax, Nova Scotia B3L 4L7
(902) 477-5621
Web site: http://www.nstu.ns.ca

Manitoba Teachers' Society
Mc Master House
191 Harcourt Street at Portage Avenue
Winnipeg, Manitoba R3J 3H2
(204) 888-7961
Web site: http://www.mbteach.org

New Brunswick Teachers' Association
P.O. Box 752
Fredericton, New Brunswick E3B 5R6
(506) 452-8921

New Brunswick Teachers' Federation
P.O. Box 1535
Fredericton, New Brunswick E3B 5G2
(506) 452-8921

Northwest Territories Teachers' Association
Box 2340
5018 48th Street
Yellowknife, Northwest Territories   X1A 2P7
(867) 873-8501

Ontario Teachers' Federation
1260 Bay Street
Suite 700
Toronto, Ontario M5R 2B5
(416) 966-3424
Web site: http://www.otffeo.on.ca

Prince Edward Island Teachers' Federation
P. O. Box 6000
Charlottetown, Prince Edward Island C1A 8B4
(902) 569-4157

Quebec Provincial Association of Teachers
17035 Brunswick Boulevard
Kirkland, Quebec H9H 5G6
(514) 694-9777

Saskatchewan Teachers' Federation
Saskatoon Office
2317 Arlington Avenue
Saskatoon, Saskatchewan S7J 2H8
(306) 373-1660
Web site: http://www.stf.sk.ca

Yukon Teachers' Association
2064 Second Avenue
Whitehorse, Yukon Y1A 1A9
(867) 668-6777

NATIONAL ORGANIZATIONS

Canadian Education Association
Suite 8-200
252 Bloor Street West
Toronto, Ontario M5S 1V5
(416) 924-7721

Canadian School Boards Association
Suite 350
130 Slater Street
Ottawa, Ontario K1P 6E2
(613) 235-3724
Web site: http://www.cdnsba.org

Canadian Teachers' Federation
110 Argyle Avenue

Ottawa, Ontario K2P 1B4
(613) 232-1505
Web site: http://www.ctf-fce.ca

SCHOOL BOARDS ASSOCIATIONS

Alberta School Boards Association
12310-105 Avenue
Edmonton, Alberta T5N 0Y4
(780) 482-7311
Web site: http://www.asba.ab.ca

British Columbia School Trustees' Association
1155 West 8th Avenue
Vancouver, British Columbia V6H 1C5
(604) 734-2721
Web site: http://www.bcsta.org

Manitoba Association of School Trustees
191 Provencher Boulevard
Winnipeg, Manitoba R2H 0G4
(204) 233-1595
Web site: http://www.mast.mb.ca
**Newfoundland and Labrador School Boards'
    Association**
The National Life Building (First Floor)
33 Pippy Place
St. John's, Newfoundland A1B 3X2
(709) 722-7171

Ontario Public School Boards Association
439 University Avenue

18th Floor
Toronto, Ontario M5G 1Y8
(416) 340-2540
Web site: http://www.opsba.org

**Prince Edward Island School Trustees
   Association**
P.O. Box 8600
Charlottetown, Prince Edward Island C1A 8V7

Quebec School Boards Association
1410 Stanley Street
Suite 515
Montreal, Quebec H3A 1P8
(514) 849-5900
Web site: http://www.qsba.qc.ca

Saskatchewan School Trustees Association
2222 Thirteenth Avenue
Suite 400
Regina, Saskatchewan S4P 3M7
(306) 569-0750
Web site: http://www.ssta.sk.ca

For Further Reading

Bosch, Karen A. and Katherine C. Kersey. *The First Year Teacher: Teaching with Confidence.* Washington, DC: National Education Association, 1994.

Deedrick, Tami. *Teachers.* Mankato, MN: Capstone Press, 1998.

Eberts, Marjorie and Margaret Gisler. *Teaching.* Lincolnwood, IL: NTC Contemporary Publishing Co., 1994.

Edelfelt, Roy A. *Careers in Education.* Lincolnwood, IL: NTC Contemporary Publishing Co. 1994.

Jonson, Kathleen F. *The New Elementary Teacher's Handbook: (Almost) Everything You Need to Know for Your First Years of Teaching.* Thousand Oaks, CA: Corwin Press, 1997.

Kane, Pearl R. (ed.). *My First Year as a Teacher: Real World Stories from America's Teachers.* New York: Signet, 1996.

Kraut, Harvey. *Teaching and the Art of Successful Classroom Management: A How-to-Guidebook for*

Teachers in Secondary Schools. Staten Island, NY: Aysa Publishing Company, 1996.

Kronowitz, Ellen L. *Your First Year of Teaching and Beyond.* White Plains, NY: Longman Publishing Group, 1996.

MacDonald, Robert E. *A Handbook for Beginning Teachers.* Reading, MA: Addison Wesley Longman, 1999.

Paoni, Frank. *On Becoming a Teacher.* Dubuque, IA: Kendall/Hunt Publishing Company, 1995.

Parkay, Forrest W. and Beverly H. Stanford. *Becoming a Teacher.* Needham Heights, MA: Allyn and Bacon, Inc., 1997.

Pelletier, Carol Marra. *A Handbook of Techniques and Strategies for Coaching Student Teachers: A Guide for Cooperating Teachers, Mentors, College Supervisors, and Teacher Educators.* Paramus, NJ: Prentice Hall, 1995.

Rubenstein, Robert E. *Hints for Teaching Success in Middle School.* Englewood, CO: Teacher Ideas Press, 1994.

Schorr, Memory Long. *A Handbook for First Year Teachers: Ready! Set! Go!* Englewood, CO: Teacher Ideas Press, 1995.

Unger, Harlow G. *Teachers and Educators.* New York: Facts on File, 1994.

Valle, Joan Della. *Teacher Career Starter.* New York: Learning Express, 1998.

Index

A
activities related to teaching, 6–8
Adult Education, 10
alternative certification, 15, 41
American Federation of Teachers, 73

B
boards of education
 local, 11, 49
 state, 11

C
career college fairs, 20
career ladders, 74, 98
career satisfaction, 2
careers
 how to begin, 44–74
 how to choose, 1–8
 surveys, 2, 4, 5
Carl D. Perkins National Direct
 Student Loan Program, 19
certification agencies, 111–121
clubs and activities, 6, 10, 80–82
colleges and universities
 admission to, 15–16, 22
 applying to, 15–16
 choosing, 14–22
 private, 14, 23–25
 state-supported, 24–25
community colleges, 14, 81
Computer Assisted Scholarships for
 Higher Education (CASH), 19
computers, 91–92, 95

contracts, 62–63, 73
Council of Chief State School
 Officers (Washington, DC), 38
credit unions, 70

D
degrees
 bachelor's, 29, 36, 41–42, 43
 master's, 12, 34, 42–43, 50, 53
 doctoral, 12, 42
disabilities, students with, 10, 93,
 97, 101–102
Discover Program, 19

E
education
 adult, 94
 bilingual, 13, 101
 business of, 9–13
 continuing, 40, 52
 cost of, 16, 22–25
 government spending on, 9–11,
 49–50
 reform in, 103–105
 special, 32, 97, 101
 specialized positions in, 92–99
 vocational, 10, 81
Educational Testing Service (ETS), 38
Education of the Handicapped, 10
education-related organizations,
 122–138
English as a Second Language
 (ESL), 13, 101

F
financial aid, 19–20, 21, 25–28
  grants, 26–27
  loans, 21, 27
  military, 19, 28
  scholarships, 21, 26, 28
  work-study programs, 27–28
fringe benefits, 65–73
  insurance, 65, 69, 72
  retirement plans, 65, 69–70, 72
  tenure, 65
  vacation and leave, 65, 70–71, 73
Future Teachers of America
  (FTA), 5, 6

G
General Equivalency Diploma
  (GED), 15
grade levels, 31–33, 75–82
grades, 4, 17, 34, 53
guidance counselors, 4–5, 15, 16,
  20, 103
Guidance Information Program
  (GIP), 19

H
Head Start, 10, 97

I
in-service teaching and training,
  41, 74
insurance, 69, 72
internships, 7
Interstate New Teachers Assessment
  and Support Consortium, 38
interviews, 59–60

J
job placement agencies, 61
job inquiry letters, 55–56
junior colleges, 14, 81

L
leaves of absence, 71, 73

lesson plans, 86–87
licensure and certification, 35–41,
  45, 75

M
mentors and mentoring, 40, 88–89
merit pay, 74

N
National Assessment of
  Educational Progress, 104
National Council for
  Accreditation of Teacher
  Education Programs, 18
National Education Association
  (NEA), 5, 73
National Teacher Examination
  (NTE), 37–38
NTE Student Program, 5
nonteaching assignments, 3, 47,
  88–90

P
parents, 4, 5, 11, 20, 89, 93, 103
Parent-Teacher Association (PTA), 11
part-time employment, 6, 18
placement offices, 54, 55
Praxis: Professional Assessments
  for Beginning Teachers, 38

R
résumés, 54, 57–58
retirement, 13, 69–70

S
salaries and benefits, 13, 42, 52,
  60–62, 63–65, 66–69, 70–74
salary subsidies, 70–71
schools
  choosing majors/minors, 30–33
  costs of, 22–25
  degree requirements of, 28–30,
    39–41
  elementary, 31–32, 78–80

high school, 32–33, 81
junior high school, 32, 80
middle school, 32, 80
nursery school, 75, 76–77
preschool, 31, 75, 76–77
private, 44, 49–50, 65
public, 44, 49–50, 65
secondary, 34–35, 47
specialists in, 92–99
types of, 46–49, 51–52
Schweitzer, Albert, 107
state departments of education, 5,
     11, 23, 35, 49
student teaching, 39, 89–90
summer jobs, 7
summer vacations, 70

T
teachers, 1–2
   aging, 13
   beginning, 39, 60
   characteristics of good teachers,
       2–3
   demand for, 13
   evaluation of, 41
   gender statistics, 12
   numbers in the US, 12, 105
   performance-based
       requirements, 39–40
   preparing to become, 14–34
   requirements for becoming,
       28–34, 83
   shortages, 13, 53–55
   tips for beginning, 62–63, 82–88
teachers' colleges, 14, 23
teacher-training programs, 13
Teach for America, 52
teaching
   abroad, 50–51
   applying for a position, 53–57, 59
   changes in profession of, 12–13,
       103–105
   choosing a job location, 44–45

choosing a position, 44–63
college, 72–73, 81–82
considering, as a career, 1–2,
     4–5, 34, 105, 107
differences between levels,
     31–33. 75–82
elementary, 31–32, 47, 78–80
emerging challenges in, 12,
     103–107
finding a position, 34, 53–63
high school, 81
junior high, 80
middle school, 80
preschool, 75–77
rewards of, 64
secondary, 32–33, 50–51
standards, 38–39, 104, 106
talented and gifted (TAG), 46
team, 46, 79
vocational, 81
technology, 95
   schools and, 91, 103
   students and, 91–92
tenure, 65
tests, 4, 19, 60
   ACT, 17
   SAT, 4, 17, 19
tips for
   building collegial relationships,
       87–88
   instruction, 86–87
   management and discipline,
       86–87
training, cost of, 22–25
tutoring, 7

U
unions, 73
U.S. Department of Education, 5

V
Vocational Education, 10
volunteer work, 6